WEST BENGAL

Sitaram Sharma began his career in journalism as Assistant Editor of a local Hindi weekly and later, as Editor of an English weekly called *Caldust*. He was also a special correspondent for *Onlooker*. He went on to become Editorial Advisor at *Business Economics*.

As Honorary Consul of Republic of Belarus, he is an active and popular member of the diplomatic corps in Kolkata. He has authored books on the United Nations and has participated in national and international conferences across the world on issues ranging from new world economic order and human rights to climate change. He was recently appointed Chairman of the Maulana Abul Kalam Azad Institute of Asian Studies, Kolkata, a centre for research on social, economic and political developments in Asia, under the Ministry of Culture of the government of India.

WEST BENGAL

CHANGING COLOURS, CHANGING CHALLENGES

SITARAM SHARMA

RUPA

First published by
Rupa Publications India Pvt. Ltd 2014
7/16, Ansari Road, Daryaganj
New Delhi 110002

Sales Centres:

Allahabad Bengaluru Chennai
Hyderabad Jaipur Kathmandu
Kolkata Mumbai

ISBN: 978-81-291-2909-3

10 9 8 7 6 5 4 3 2 1

Typeset by RECTO GRAPHICS, Delhi

Dedicated to

Advita, Sangini, Ananya, Lavanya,
Malvika, Payal-Abhishek, Pooja-Anupam,
Kadambari-Amit and Asha;
you will share more of my heart and mind
now that the writing of this book is finally over.
And to the memory of my parents
Savitri and Dwarkadas

Contents

Foreword

When she was India's high commissioner in London, Vijayalakshmi Pandit told students at a British university of a visit she paid to the University of California at Berkeley as president of the United Nations General Assembly. 'We have a wonderful girl from India studying here,' the vice-chancellor gushed on receiving her. 'I wish you could have met her but she's away today.' Impressed and intrigued by his enthusiasm, Mrs Pandit asked if the girl topped her class. No, said the vice-chancellor reluctantly, but she really was remarkably talented. Was she then an outstanding athlete, Mrs Pandit wanted to know, an exceptional musician or a dedicated social worker? In each case, the increasingly embarrassed vice-chancellor murmured a hesitant denial. 'But she must be good at something for you to recommend her so warmly?' Mrs Pandit insisted. Well, said the vice-chancellor after some reflection, she's a very good debater. 'That's not an ability,' Mrs Pandit retorted, 'that's a national liability!'

I am sure the girl was Bengali although Mrs Pandit didn't say so. If Bengalis are the most afflicted with the gift of the gab, it's probably because we had a head start over most other Indians in the business of coming to grips with modernity. A stable administration, the rule of law and Macaulay's famous or infamous (depending on your position in the political firmament) Minute on education built on India's native intellectual heritage to shape Amartya Sen's 'argumentative Indian' and develop the 'heterodoxy and dialogue' that others can find so confusing.

Every so often volatile and loquacious Bengal—surely the West has long been redundant?—quickens to the breaking of another dawn. Colours change, as Sitaram Sharma's title proclaims, but '*plus ça change, plus c'est la même chose*—the more things change, the more they stay the same.'

A thrill of expectation animated the crowds that swarmed into the Legislative Assembly in March 1967 when the first United Front came to power. Only eight months later the Communist speaker, Bijoy Banerjee, surprised everyone with a display of colonial erudition and compared governor Dharma Vira's arbitrary dismissal of an elected government with the actions of England's King Charles I some 320 years earlier. The Left seemed handsomely vindicated 10 years later when Jyoti Basu, whom Sharma compares to China's Deng Xiaoping, became chief minister. But if Kerala made history in 1957 by appointing the world's first democratically elected Communist government, Bengal made history in 2011 by democratically dismissing the Marxist-led Left Front after thirty-four years in office.

Jolly Mohan Kaul, who joined the undivided Communist Party of India 'in search of a better world', the title of his own memoirs, attributes the Marxists' defeat to 'their volte face from being champions of the poor, the workers and the peasants, to becoming protectors and promoters of the interests of the richer sections of society.' He might also have mentioned that in 1970 another state governor, Shanti Swarup Dhawan, incurred the business elite's enmity by saying he would far rather trust his daughter to a Calcutta—as it still was before phoney and frivolous nationalism took over—taxi than to one in Delhi. The National Crime Records Board records that by 2013 Bengal lost that innocence to account for 12.67 per cent of the country's sex crimes. The reinvented

Kolkata became India's third most unsafe city for women. And this under Bengal's first woman chief minister, Mamata Banerjee, who has a Cabinet, says Sharma pertly, but no colleagues.

No one any longer says with Gopal Krishna Gokhale that what Bengal thinks today, India thinks tomorrow. Even fewer agree that the King-Emperor George V was right to predict when announcing the transfer of India's capital to Delhi that Calcutta would always remain the country's commercial hub. History has not been kind to the state or the city. But that has not affected Bengal's exuberant political life which is chronicled in these pages.

Whether or not this exuberance serves any concrete purpose is another matter. But, traditionally, politics is of the essence of existence for most Bengalis. E.M. Forster's comment about Indians in *Two Cheers for Democracy* applies—or used to apply—especially to Bengalis. 'You cannot understand the modern Indians unless you realise that politics occupy them passionately and constantly, that artistic problems, and even social problems—yes, and even economic problems—are subsidiary,' Forster wrote. 'Their attitude is "first we must find the correct political solution and then we can deal with other matters."'

Despite the supporting evidence of Bengali literature, of its vibrant theatre, of violence between gangs sporting different political colours, of bureaucratic and police partisanship, union and student turbulence and the endless public rallies that choke the streets of Jawaharlal Nehru's city of processions, some might argue there hasn't been enough real politics since Bengalis ceased to count in Bengal. The absence of substantive issues may also explain his grandson's jibe about a dying city. We might have to look elsewhere for serious political activity tailored to defined objectives, good or bad. Not since the partition of 1905 has Bengal experienced either the passion and earnestness that marked Punjab's determined campaign to compensate and rehabilitate refugees from erstwhile West Pakistan, Tamil Nadu's frenzied resistance to Hindi, Uttar Pradesh's demonic destruction of the Babri Masjid, Gujarat's communal killing fields or Maharashtra's attacks on outsiders. Sarat Chandra Bose's vision of sovereign unity failed to capture Bengal's popular imagination. New Delhi's rejection of Siddhartha Shankar Ray's proposal for six growth centres to foster industry, create jobs and revitalize the state's economy provoked not a murmur.

There was only the empty roller-coaster excitement of what Bengal's former finance minister, Ashok Mitra, 'a self-confessed Marxist', dismisses as 'playing-at-politics'. The drama of massive gatherings flaunting flaming torches to the strains of the Internationale on Kolkata's Maidan, intense sessions over endless cups of tea in dingy tea shops or Mamata Banerjee's tirades against Maoists, Marxists and Congress don't add up to more than inconsequential *adda*. There might be a catchy peg like the Tram Bus Fare Enhancement Resistance Committee or a rhyme without reason like the '*Amar naam, tomar naam, Vietnam, Vietnam*' chant that could grind the city to a halt. But the excuses for boisterousness are trivial or remote.

Kanu Sanyal's suicide highlighted both the failure of politics and the politics of failure. His Naxalites were never within *paan*-spitting distance of the countryside rising to encircle and overpower Kolkata. Now, it would seem that Chhattisgarh has stolen Bengal's revolutionary thunder. What passes for political debate here is public theatrics and a conversational free-for-all unattached to any cause to nourish the soul or heal the body. The popular cry of '*Inquilab Zindabad!*' has neither meaning nor resonance.

If history is 'past politics', to quote Sir John Seeley, the 19th Century English essayist and historian, there's rich fare to mull over, from devotional fervour and terrorism to the flourish of a leading

Bengali-owned English-language newspaper's quaint heading, 'Dauntless Dinesh Dies at Dawn', marking the heroism of the legendary trio after whom Dalhousie Square was renamed. Henry Derozio's Bengal Renaissance and the rousing rhetoric associated with Surendranath (Surrender Not) Banerjea belongs to that past. But if politics is 'present history', to quote Seeley again, future generations may find the chronicles of our time very barren. Basu's 'historic blunder' eclipses the tragedy of Marichjhapi; Nandigram is a talking point, but the magnitude of illegal immigration and Bengal's changing demography don't appear to merit more than a shrug. Mamata Banerjee suspects a conspiracy to unseat her behind every bush.

Sitaram Sharma has enjoyed a ringside view of these stirring and not so stirring events. As a journalist, he noticed minutiae like who sat where on public occasions or who spoke to whom, and drew his own political conclusions. Like many journalists, he has occasionally been a player. More often, he has been an observer and chronicler. Reading these pages, one is not certain where vocation ends and avocation begins. He is a businessman, an honorary member of the city's consular corps and an activist in the United Nations movement. He is living proof, too, of the catholicity that enabled Mamata Banerjee to boast that Marwaris are as Bengali as she is.

The Changing Colours of his title signifies Bengal's refusal to be tied eternally to one political loyalty. But the sequence of events he describes is a reminder that political power as an end in itself does not generate vision, constructive thinking or a commitment to growth. His analysis warns against the all-too-common blame game and reminds us that 'not everything depends on the Centre or on land; not everything can be explained away by competently prepared excuses'. It also indicates that the people must be held as responsible as politicians for the dawns that periodically illumine

Bengal's skies always turning out to be false. Sharma illustrates the state's work ethic (or lack of it) by repeating the Coffee House crack that government employees would demand overtime if revolution occurs after 5 p.m.

When the Left Front's days seemed numbered, this writer wondered, like some others perhaps, whether the change would not take Bengal from the frying pan into the fire. That fear has not yet been set at rest. There is no doubt that Bengal yearns for a better life. There is no doubt either that if Bengal is to regain its place in the sun, adversarial politics will have to give way to positive cooperation. What Mitra called playing-at-politics is no substitute for serious political action by a party with a well-defined vision of the future, wise leadership, disciplined manpower, mass support and a strategy for achieving its reconstruction plan within a stipulated time frame. Bengal is still waiting for the *poriborton*, change, that was promised in 2011.

Sunanda K. Datta-Ray

Preface

A Ringside View

As I write these lines, West Bengal has changed from 'red' to 'green'. Or has it? Was it really red in 2011? It was certainly not a red of the same hue that I saw in 1977, the year that marked the unprecedented success of the Communist Party of India (Marxist)-led Left Front in the Assembly elections, winning 231 seats in a house of 294. The results surprised all, including the CPI(M), which won an absolute majority, securing 178 seats on its own. Over the years, through successive Assembly elections, it had changed from red to pink, after which it darkened inexplicably to black until the 2011 elections, by which time, the red was hardly discernible.

The red here is more than a colour—it connotes an entire philosophy. Even the most ardent supporters of the Left Front amongst the intelligentsia were flabbergasted by the grim shade that the ruling party had acquired. It had changed significantly from five decades ago when, in 1962, I first stepped into the public arena as a teenager.

The era of coalition politics had arrived in West Bengal in 1967, as in the rest of India, and governments began to be made up of different combinations of factions. Parties began to split and the splinter groups faded or merged into other groups in a massive churning of the political order, until 1977, when the Left came to power in West Bengal. Thus began the long reign of the Left Front: it promised stability as it continued to return after each election until it seemed it would remain in control forever.

Yet it did not. Over all these years, I have followed the changing political scene and even been a part of it. Occasionally, I watched from the outside but by a fortunate combination of circumstances, I secured a ringside view of the proceedings. I deliberately avoided being at the centre stage. I venture to think that, while watching from the wings, I have occasionally been able to exert some influence to the course of events.

In any event, I have been in close contact with most of the leading political personalities in the state and at the centre, thanks to my early years as a political activist and journalist and later as a peace activist. These positions have afforded me the opportunity to observe and study the nuances of the political shifts taking place, and also to interact closely with those at the helm of affairs and those striving to come into power.

Since it was idealism that stoked my interest in politics and it was never my intention to become an active politician, I have been able to take a more objective view of developments than one who wished to make it a career. Even journalism was more of a mission than profession for me. Thus, when a friend connected to the publishing industry suggested that I write a book on the changing political scene in West Bengal, I was eager to pen my experiences.

I hope this account, encompassing the last half-century or so, will be of some use to those trying to understand the complexities of the socioeconomic and political environment prevailing in this state that is so full of potential; that is vibrant at all times but one that sets its own rhythm, often refusing to march to the beat of the global drum. The goddess Saraswati continues to hold sway over the masses far more than her sibling Lakshmi does. Political or social debates continue to be better informed and sharper than the dialogue around industrial development, even though West Bengal, more than most other states needs employment; needs development, as I understand it. Yet there are those who believe in development under a different paradigm to the one that holds sway in this day and age of globalization.

If the pages that follow make some contribution, however small, to enabling an understanding of West Bengal; the minds of those who people it and contribute to the progress of the state that, despite its tremendous potential, has turned from a leader into a laggard, my effort will not have been in vain.

Sitaram Sharma

The Rise and the Fall

O! What a fall was there, my countrymen!

—William Shakespeare, *Julius Caesar*

'They have lost touch with the ground reality and election results will prove that.' The tones were hushed and there was cautious expectation in the air. These were no mere punters but Kolkata diplomats at their business session at the Taj Bengal. It was Wednesday, 11 May 2011; the West Bengal Assembly election results were only two days away. Several city-based diplomats were at their regular monthly luncheon meeting, hosted by the Consular Corps of Kolkata. Vladimir V. Lazarev, Consul-General of the Russian Federation and Dean of the Consular Corps, welcomed the chief guest, Ravindra Kumar, managing director and chief editor of the *The Statesman* and introduced the new Consul-General of Germany, Rainer Schmiedchen, who had assumed his duties only a day earlier.

The proceedings were overshadowed by whispers about the forthcoming election results. It was unusual for foreign policy experts to evince so much interest in any election other than the national polls. It did not take much to sense the pulse of the electorate but no one wanted to say it out loud: the Left was out. On the day the election results were out, Friday, 13 May, the same diplomat rang up to say, 'India is not going to witness another anti-nuclear movement in a hurry.' His observation was a subtle comment on the Left's role during the protracted negotiations for the Indo-US nuclear deal. My wicked mind went back to the alleged role of the US's Central Intelligence Agency (CIA) in the internal affairs of sovereign countries during the Cold War era.

The point was that the diplomatic corps, which had resigned itself to a red rule in West Bengal in perpetuity, was agog with expectations of change. A victory for Mamata Banerjee would be monumental for Bengal and globally significant, as was later proved by the visit of the US Secretary of State, Hillary Clinton, to Kolkata to meet the new chief minister. The feisty lady of the masses, uprooting the communists from the state, would change the way the world would look at West Bengal.

To go back in time, in 1977, when the Left unexpectedly swept the polls, the title of the lead story of the English weekly *Caldust*, which I was then editing, was 'Bengal Goes Red'. I still remember a faint smile on the face of the never-smiling Jyoti Basu when he saw it. Fast forward to 2011. Shortly before the elections, even before a single vote had been cast, I saw what I consider one of the best cover story titles of the period carried by *India Today* (28 March 2011): 'Mamata's Green Revolution in Red Land', predicting the rout of the Left Front after thirty-four years of rule in West Bengal.

Indeed, when the defeat of the Left Front in West Bengal became a reality, some even likened it to the fall of the Berlin Wall. They called it 'the fall of the Bengal wall'. To compare the two events that took place in different parts of the world and in circumstances that were very different might be somewhat facetious, though there is no doubt that the fall of the Left Front in 2011, since its meteoric rise in 1977, was an event of great significance. It may well turn out to be a turning point in the post-independence political history of the state and the country. It may also turn out to be a damp squib unless the new rulers quickly master the art of governance.

Governance for whom? This is a question to which no satisfactory answer has been provided by sociologists or pundits, because the Bengali mind presents a curious conundrum. Even in an increasingly market-oriented world, the Bengali sets more store by culture. Accomplishment is not necessarily measured by income—though money power counts for a great deal, especially in a state where '*paaiyay debaar rajiniti*' (the politics of securing benefits for underlings) has been the key to many vote banks. Almost everywhere, benefits that should come to the citizen as a matter of right can only be received through the intermediation of a powerful middleman, usually allied to the party in power. The average Bengali cannot be bothered to contest this social arrangement.

Yet the average Bengali is neither unaware nor is he daft. An inadequately appointed school for his child; a road that has not been repaired for ages; an officially electrified village that does not receive power—the average Bengali learns to improvise and make do. One would imagine that his senses have been bludgeoned into passivity over years of dispossession. That is not quite true though.

The Bengali is almost always witty—nothing is as clever as the wall posters that rival political parties prepare; compassionate—witness the alacrity with which the *paara* (neighbourhood) boy will come to one's help; enterprising when it suits him; interested—newspapers are most closely read and political issues hotly debated in many forums and every street corner *adda* (group gossip); and he is almost always culturally gifted. The surfeit of talent on show from Bengal on numerous television contests bears testimony to this.

The Bengali is also intensely proud of his Bengaliness, and considers himself to be a cut above the rest of the country in terms of intelligence and cultural sophistication. The Bengali has happily relinquished the position of entrepreneurial leadership to people from other states. While there is small time enterprise in the hands of local entrepreneurs, Bengali-led industry is significant by its scarcity. The average Bengali is also quite comfortable with the state's relative backwardness in comparison to the advances that other states have made in terms of the accepted development paradigm.

Only when he feels pushed into a corner does the average Bengali react. They rose in action against the British Raj and provided many leaders for the freedom movement. Later, the intelligentsia rose against social oppression as an entire generation of youth took to Naxalism in the 1960s and '70s. And finally, the Bengali rose against the entrenched oppression of the Left Front that the people of the state had once supported in the hope that a party committed to communist philosophy would take care of the average Bengali's interest. The bottomline is that Bengal is unique and good governance in Bengal must also be uniquely suited to this state.

Mamata Banerjee, who rose to occupy the political leadership space that had long been vacated by the only other political opponent to the Left, the Congress, ensured that she fitted the image of a culturally conscious leader, who could recite poetry and paint with an élan that was equal to her oratory skills and the intrepid challenges she threw to the Left. She ensured that she appealed to the Bengali intelligentsia as much as she did to the farmers—whose cause she espoused—to create the foundation for her electoral success. She has consciously made herself a part of the cricket-crazy crowds at Eden Gardens alongside Shahrukh Khan—the film star who is the brand ambassador of the state—and is at home bursting into Tagore's songs. She is at once the people's *didi* (elder sister) and the champion of the dispossessed in her bid to appeal to her vote banks. Mamata Banerjee knew whom she had to have by her side when she went to the polls.

The Left's support base—mainly the farmers and the working class—had already been eroded over years; the Left seemed to be its own worst enemy, largely due to a steady erosion in the class orientation of the Left front Government, even to the extent of being neoliberal. It was left to Mamata Banerjee to feed on the widespread revulsion for the Left, take the Congress along for whatever little benefits that it could offer and get virtually every Bengali icon to campaign for her. She even had the ultimate icon of the leftists, Jyoti Basu, demonstrating his affection for her. Mamata had captivated the Bengali psyche, one that represented years of struggle—against the Raj, against the destabilizing effects of partition in the 1940s and then the next influx of refugees in the '70s. It encompassed bitterness at years of 'step-motherly' treatment by the centre as it watched the symbols of its richness during the Raj get virtually decimated due to flight of capital during the license-permit era because of discriminatory policies followed by the Central Government towards West Bengal. Yet it was a psyche that swelled with pride at the sight of the mighty Howrah Bridge spanning the Hooghly or the Ochterlony Monument that stood tall over the green expanse of the Maidan.

A complex psyche, indeed. Mamata arrived at a time that this psyche desperately needed healing. These were the people that Mamata Banerjee had to govern even as she strategized how to benefit from the reforming culture evident in other parts of India.

Refugees are for Keeps

> Long years ago we made a tryst with destiny, and now the time comes when we shall redeem our pledge, not wholly or in full measure, but very substantially. At the stroke of the midnight hour, when the world sleeps, India will awake to life and freedom. A moment comes, which comes but rarely in history, when we step out from the old to the new, when an age ends, and when the soul of a nation, long suppressed, finds utterance. It is fitting that at this solemn moment, we take the pledge of dedication to the service of India and her people and to the still larger cause of humanity.
>
> —Jawaharlal Nehru at the midnight session of the Constituent Assembly, 14-15 August 1947

August 16, 1946, will long be remembered as a black day. It was the date selected by Mohammad Ali Jinnah to give the call for 'Direct Action', the overt political purpose of which was to mobilize the Muslim community behind the demand for Pakistan to be carved out of the India then ruled by the British. On 16 August, massive riots broke out in Calcutta and the surrounding regions. Within 72 hours, more than 6,000 people lost their lives. Some estimates place the final toll at 10,000 in Calcutta alone.

The Calcutta riots were significant in more ways than one. Even though they had been started by the Muslim League as a deliberate ploy to buttress Jinnah's demand for Pakistan, the Muslim population, a minority in the city, was very soon at the receiving end of the violence that erupted. This acted as a trigger that set off a chain reaction, which has been well described in an army memo quoted by Ramachandra Guha in one of his articles in the *Telegraph*: 'Calcutta was revenged in Noakhali, Noakhali in Bihar, Bihar in Gurmukteswar, Gurmukteswar in?' The rioting and the violence did not stop with the announcement of the transfer of power.

Indeed, the violence that broke out after the partition of Punjab was perhaps unprecedented in history. An equally tragic consequence of the August 1946 violence, however, has been the use of the riots and mass violence as a political weapon, which is a continuing feature of the socio-political environment of the country till this day. It is pertinent to quote C. Rajagopalachari, the Governor of Bengal who warned, on 4 September 1947, that 'Refugees are being sent all over India. They will scatter communal hatred on a wide scale and will churn up enormous ill-will everywhere. Refugees have to be looked after but we have to take steps to prevent the infection of hatred beyond the necessary minimum, which cannot be prevented.'

Born on 13 August 1946, I was spared a personal experience of the tragedy and the horrors of the riots but they left their mark on the psyche of a whole generation who had witnessed the events that started in August 1946 and continued well into the late 1940s. With partition, millions of refugees came to India both from East and West Pakistan. I have childhood memories of this. I was born in a village called Kalanaur, in the district of Rohtak, then in Punjab, which underwent an almost total transfer of population with Muslims in the area going to West Pakistan and Hindus from West Punjab arriving as refugees or '*sharanarthis*'. Millions of refugees had crossed over from East Bengal (then East Pakistan) to West Bengal and the other border states of Assam and Tripura.

Following the partition of India, the largest mass migration in history took place. According to some estimates, based on the 1951 census of displaced persons, about 14.5 million people crossed the border from the two parts of the newly-formed state of Pakistan to India and from India to Pakistan. Nearly 80 per cent of this migration took place from West Pakistan into the western part of India and the rest from East Pakistan into eastern India. The figures for the transfer in the east were 3.5 million Hindus from East Pakistan into West Bengal, Tripura and Assam in India. A little less than a million (0.7 million) Muslims crossed over to East Pakistan.

These figures represent the migration that took place immediately after the partition but while the transfer took place at one go in the west, it was a gradual process in the east, starting from immediately before the partition, developing into a massive exodus immediately after and then continuing in a steady stream for many years. The discontent was further heightened as comparisons started being made between the steps being taken for the relief and rehabilitation of the refugees from West Pakistan and those being taken for the refugees streaming into West Bengal.

With the exception of a few, relatively affluent people, who had migrated just before August 1947 and had taken care to make arrangement for the sale or exchange of property with Muslims in West Bengal, the others came with just the little that they could physically carry. The administration, overwhelmed by the unexpected influx, was totally unprepared and could do little by way of providing shelter or relief in cash or kind. Finding no other alternative, the refugees initially took shelter on the platforms of Sealdah and other railway stations in West Bengal.

The picture in the west was different. The transfer was not only on a far more massive scale, it was one of the bloodiest in history. The number of those killed on either side ran into thousands; the exact number will perhaps never be known. Those arriving across the border into India knew that there was no hope of their returning to their homes and the government in India, too, had realized that the refugees had come to stay. In the east, as the transfer of population had been relatively less bloody, a considerable number of Hindus remained in East Pakistan and so did a large number of Muslims in West Bengal. This made the administration in India feel that the influx of refugees in the east was a temporary phenomenon and only temporary arrangements were made for their rehabilitation initially.

It was this difference in the nature of the migration that resulted in a massive exercise to provide shelter and to give relief in the west. The hordes fleeing from the terror entered India and were directed by the government to a refugee camp in Kurukshetra (then in Punjab, now in Haryana). A vast city of tents emerged on the plain to house waves of migrants, sometimes up to 20,000 a day. The camp was initially planned for 100,000 refugees but it came to accommodate more than three times that number.

Most of the refugees from West Pakistan were farmers and so were most of the Muslims who migrated there from Punjab. Although the land left behind in west Punjab was as much as 2.7 million hectares as against 1.9 abandoned by the farmers in East Punjab and the land in the west had much better irrigation facilities compared to the land in the east, the farmers, mainly Sikhs, set to work with characteristic ingenuity and enterprise, digging new wells, building new houses and planting their crops. By 1950, the countryside was alive once again.

Compared to this, immigration into Bengal was chiefly of the *bhadralok*: professionals, lawyers and teachers, along with workers, artisans and those working on the land. The administration did not have the advantage of land abandoned by farmers. There was no clear-cut policy with regard to rehabilitation and so the refugees took possession of empty houses while others colonized vacant land along roads and railway lines as well as freshly cleared shrub jungle and freshly drained marshes, forcing the refugees to take the law into their own hands.

The problem of refugees who had come from East Pakistan was complicated by the fact that, till quite late, neither the state nor the centre had quite realized the nature of the crisis that was staring them in the face. They were lulled into a false sense of comfort, believing that since the refugees would return, there was no question of making permanent arrangements for their rehabilitation. The Congress in West Bengal believed that the refugees should be encouraged to go back and those in East Pakistan who were planning to come over should be persuaded to stay away.

A news item published on 12 October 1947 headlined 'Exodus from E. Bengal; Dr Ghosh Discourages Move' stated that, 'In an interview yesterday (Saturday) Dr Prafulla Chandra Ghosh, Prime Minister, West Bengal (that was how the Chief Minister was then designated), said: "We do not want exodus. But if in spite of that anybody comes it will be the business of the people and the State to help them as much as possible."' Significantly, Dr Ghosh used the word 'anybody', indicating that he was not expecting mass migration.

A letter to the editor of the *Amrita Bazar Patrika* dated 8 April 1948 reflects the anguish of the writer at the plight of those who had already crossed the border. He writes, 'There seems to be a widespread underrating of the problems of the refugees from Eastern Pakistan who are more than 2.5 millions, who are being forced to migrate to West Bengal because of the communal fanaticism of a theocratic state [...] have lost all means of livelihood in the process of migration [...] and are destitutes (sic) who badly need shelter, food, clothing and means of livelihood. Ghosh's Ministry in West Bengal because of its callousness, incompetence and lack of foresight was conspicuous by its systematic denial of the problems of the refugees from Eastern Pakistan nor did it not even apprise the Central Government of the immensity of the problem…' He went on to state that migration from East Pakistan had come to stay and instead of what was likely to be a disorderly migration, there should be a planned evacuation.

A perusal of the available documents and media reports of the period clearly confirms this position. It was the government's attitude that resulted in a very callous and ineffective programme for the rehabilitation of refugees, whose numbers kept increasing and, by the 1960s, had crossed five million. This explains the somewhat warped psyche of the refugees and their resentment against the centre and the Congress governments in the state and their opting for the Communists, who appeared to be the only viable opposition at that time.

The inept handling of the refugee problem in West Bengal and the general lack of awareness of the situation prevailing in the state are reflected in an interesting incident that occurred in 1983. I had led a delegation of the West Bengal Federation of United Nations Associations to call on the then President of India, Zail Singh, at Raj Bhavan in Calcutta. The delegation included B.R. Chakravarty of the IAS, secretary of the refugee and rehabilitation department of the government of West Bengal. When the secretary was introduced to the President, the latter looked startled and said, 'Do you still have a refugee department in West Bengal? In Punjab and even at the centre it has long been wound up. What do you do? Do you still have refugees to be rehabilitated?' Chakravarty was highly embarrassed and mumbled something about the lack of resources and the reluctance of the refugees to be sent out of the state by way of explanation that could hardly have convinced the president.

Meanwhile, in West Bengal, an All-Bengal Refugee Council of Action was formed in early 1948. Processions and demonstrations were organized. Shouting the slogan *'Aamra Kahara Bastuhar'*, (Who are we? We are destitute), the demonstrators often turned violent. Faced with tear gas shells, lathicharges and occasional bullets, they burnt trams, cars and buses. Frequent clashes became a feature of life in Calcutta. On the outskirts of the city, the protesters forcibly occupied fallow or marshy land wherever they found vacant open areas.

On these they built what came to be called squatter colonies, clusters of huts with thatched, tiled or corrugated iron roofs, bamboo-mat walls and mud floors. Committees were formed to carry on the administration of these colonies and there was continuous agitation, demanding regularization of the colonies. This was a demand that the government not only refused to meet but, instead, made repeated attempts to reclaim the occupied land and to forcibly evict the squatters. Pitched battles were fought night after night with women taking the lead with sticks and whatever other weapons they could lay their hands on, and with sheer force of numbers and organized resistance, forced the police to retreat.

The Communists took the lead in this matter and, in the course of the struggle, the refugees threw up some of the party's best cadres. An important feature of these colonies was the role played by women cadres. In almost all the major colonies, Mahila Samitis (women's groups) sprang up, led by Communist women cadres. These were broad-based committees, which included those without political affiliation or with affiliation to other Left parties and even Congress sympathizers, who worked shoulder to shoulder with their sisters for sheer survival.

Those who were unable to find vacant land to occupy continued in 'camps' for years, surviving on the dole given by the government.

Conditions in some of these camps were appalling. Communist influence in these camps too was growing as they organized and participated in agitations and protest actions, which often led to clashes with the police. Since the administrative headquarters of the government department in charge of relief and rehabilitation was in Delhi, it was naturally more involved with the work related to the refugees in the west and had little interest in the problems of refugees from East Bengal. With the task of rehabilitation of the refugees in the west completed, the department was wound up. However, there is still a refugee, relief and rehabilitation department in West Bengal.

I was too young to be directly involved in the refugee movement at its peak in the 1950s and early '60s but felt its impact on the political and social environment of West Bengal and Calcutta as I matured. If the economy of the state gradually declined and the city's infrastructure started deteriorating, this was undoubtedly in large part due to the sudden influx of millions of refugees.

This accentuated the food problem, which became acute when there was a succession of droughts in the late 1950s. It exacerbated the unemployment problem and did a lot of damage to the environment of the city. The frustration of the unemployed youth, the widening gap between the rich and poor combined with inflation and food scarcity was a lethal combination that was bound to spawn extremist trends.

It helped to strengthen and spread the Left and extreme Left movements in Bengal. Anyone growing up and studying in Calcutta, particularly in college, could not but be influenced by the refugee movement and take note of the resultant leftward swing of the political movement. To that extent, it definitely had an impact on me. I was already beginning to take an interest in politics, particularly after I joined City College, having been initiated through a demonstration protesting against the Chinese aggression. I was also involved with a 'study group', a city-based group of intellectuals, in organizing major processions against Indonesia for poking its nose in and supporting Pakistan during the Indo-Pak war of 1965.

I had direct contact with the refugees later, in the early 1970s when 10 million refugees fled from East Pakistan (now Bangladesh) and sought shelter in West Bengal to escape the brutal repression of the Pakistan government. Most of them sought to stay in West Bengal while some migrated to Assam and Tripura. I visited a few refugee camps to experience firsthand the conditions there. The plight of the refugees was heart-rending. Even though many NGOs were involved in relief work with generous funding from the government of India, the enormity of the refugee influx was such that it was difficult for the administration to cope with it.

As journalists, my friends and I investigated some reliable leads about financial bungling by certain relief societies and published the story in our Hindi weekly, *Jan Sansar*. As soon as the story was published there was panic among many relief societies. An old and reputed relief society convened an emergency meeting and, after realizing what was going on, promptly decided to refund a huge amount to the government. The government also avoided making a noise.

This exposure to the plight of refugees indirectly in early life and directly, later, left a lasting impression on me and led to an important programme being initiated by the organization with which I have been involved for many years, the West Bengal Federation of United Nations Associations (WEBFUNA). Since 1997, I have organized an annual inter-school debate on the plight and rights of the refugees jointly with UNHCR (United Nations High Commissioner of Refugees) and *The Statesman Voices* on behalf of WEBFUNA. I recall the chief of mission of the UNHCR in Delhi, Augustin Mahiga, visiting Kolkata and calling upon the state's refugee and rehabilitation minister at Writers' Building. To his utter bewilderment, the minister said that he was a refugee and I had to explain that what the minister meant was that he had come as a refugee at the time of India's partition.

The deep scars that the partition has left on the psyche of those who were its actual victims and even those who have come into contact with them get reflected in the debates that WEBFUNA has held on the subject. Some of the participants have been the children of those who came as refugees, and others have heard about their plight and their struggle to rehabilitate themselves. In their speeches the students reveal an awareness of the problems of the refugees and eloquently express their empathy for them. The subjects of debate have ranged from 'Refugees are an unwanted burden' to 'Once a refugee, always a refugee'. An article by Abhishek Mukherjee, winner of the first prize at the inter-school debate held in 1999 was even published in *The Statesman* on 20 January 2000.

The sheer emotional tragedy of the huge influx of refugees before and immediately after the partition and the even bigger influx during the second wave that came during the 1971 war with Pakistan was worsened by the financial implications that the influx had for the state. Even more important, it changed the demography of the region and a census today might well show that nearly half the population of West Bengal comprises those who have their origins in different districts of the erstwhile East Bengal, now Bangladesh. This has had its impact on West Bengal politics as well.

Within a few months of the transfer of power in 1947, Mahatma Gandhi was assassinated. Partition not only altered the geography of the subcontinent—it had a deep and lasting impact on the psyche of the people of both countries and on the political and economic conditions of the region. In this respect, the effect was perhaps more severe in Bengal than in Punjab. As one has seen, the Punjab exodus comprised mainly farmers but the Bengal refugees were a mixed lot.

Calcutta had been the commercial capital of India in British times. In fact, till 1911 it had also been the political capital and the seat of administration for the whole of India. Jute, tea and coal were the major industries here. Engineering firms had also come up to service the needs of the railways and, during the war, for supplies to the armed forces. Most of them were owned and managed by British managing agencies, which had their headquarters in Calcutta. The indigenous business community comprising the Marwaris and some Gujaratis had mainly been in trade following the announcement of the transfer of power. However, many factories owned by the managing agencies saw a transfer of ownership to the wealthy indigenous business families.

It was while all this was happening that I was growing up in Calcutta. Our family had migrated from Punjab in the 1910s. My father Dwarkadas Sharma came to Calcutta and went into business starting a brokerage firm. I went to the Daulatram Nopany Vidyalaya—made famous in recent years by its illustrious alumnus, Lakshmi Mittal—and then joined the City College, graduating in 1967. I went on to do my MBA from the Indian Institute of Social Welfare and Business Management.

I recall that my MBA certificate was signed by the former chief minister of West Bengal, Prafulla Chandra Sen, then president of the institute. Among my classmates was S. K. Roy of the well-known Peerless Company and others who later became prominent in various fields. I was simultaneously enrolled for law in the Calcutta University Law College, where Dr Pratap Chandra Chunder who later became union education minister, was my teacher. I passed the preliminary and intermediate exams but did not sit for the finals as

I had decided to focus on the MBA. All this time, the political scene in Calcutta was teeming with activity and no one could remain untouched by the political currents.

I was only sixteen and still in school when the Chinese attacked the country in 1962. I was drawn into meetings and cultural programmes to rouse patriotic sentiments and to collect cash and other materials in kind for the Prime Minister's National Defence Fund. This was through the Bal Parishad, a local organization of children and youth. My brush with politics continued in 1963 when, at 17, I was drafted as a volunteer for a 'thinkers convention' at Mahajati Sadan, Calcutta, which was addressed by Prime Minister Jawaharlal Nehru. I was deputed to the first floor balcony, rather far from the stage and I might have had to rest content with seeing and hearing from afar.

Luck came my way, however. While I was standing on the balcony, there was a sudden commotion and, lo and behold, I found Pandit Nehru approaching the lobby on the first floor escorted by Lady Ranu Mukherjee. This was not in the scheduled programme and must have happened because Lady Ranu wanted to show him something, probably a painting or some other work of art on the first floor.

Full of excitement, I, along with others, rushed towards him and all that I remember is that I was able to shake hands with him before he was escorted back to the hall downstairs where the chief minister was waiting for him. Half of what I heard of Pandit Nehru's speech from the balcony was lost in the excitement of shaking hands with him and I was dying to tell my friends about it. How much that touch meant in terms of inspiring a young man to stay politically interested I have never assessed but it did mean much more than a handshake.

The Leftward Swing

From each according to his ability,
To each according to his needs.

—Karl Marx

The influx of refugees after the partition was, however, only one of the many factors that led to the leftward swing that ultimately catapulted the United Front to power in 1967 and again in 1969. On both these occasions, the coalition governments formed with the Left as the main constituent were dismissed by the central government under Article 356 of the Constitution. This Article has acquired quite some notoriety due to its alleged misuse. The essence of the Article is that in the case of a certain defined state of affairs, as ascertained and reported by the governor of the state concerned, the President may conclude that the 'constitutional machinery' in the state has failed. Thereupon, the President makes a 'Proclamation of Emergency', dismissing the state legislature and executive.

During a state of emergency, the President is vested with tremendous discretionary powers. Article 355 states: It shall be the duty of the union to protect every state against external aggression and internal disturbance and to ensure that the government of every state is carried on in accordance with the provisions of this Constitution.

How did things come to such a pass in West Bengal that the Congress had to resort to such a drastic method to counter the Left?

The answer lies largely in the tectonic shifts caused by the refugee influx and the unrest on account of the food scarcity that cast a pall of gloom across the countryside. West Bengal in the late 1950s and '60s was like a powder keg waiting to explode. A number of leftist movements swept the state, one after another, eroding the support base of the Congress. All were handled ineptly by the administration. The most important of these movements was the food movement but there were others, such as the movement against the increase in tram fares, the teachers' movement and the movement against the proposal to merge West Bengal and Bihar.

The story of the rise of the Left parties in West Bengal begins with the disintegration and decline of the Congress both at the centre and in the state. The two are interlinked. The organizational stalwarts in the Congress party had started attacking Prime Minister Indira Gandhi as early as 1966. The leaders were busy dividing the loaves and fishes of office; they had forgotten to keep tabs on the mood of the people. The Congress faced a setback in the 1967 Parliamentary polls with a reduced majority of 283 out of a total of 520 in the Lok Sabha. In West Bengal, the Congress was thrown out of power altogether.

The Left promised a pro-worker, pro-peasant agenda of action and a better and more stable government after a decade of instability. The Congress-led governments, headed by Bidhan Chandra Roy and Prafulla Chandra Sen, had alienated the masses with their handling of the spiraling unrest over crippling food scarcity and the famine. Their 'management by muzzling' completed their alienation from the masses.

The present generation that grew up seeing the unpleasing face of the Left Front will find it difficult to believe that the victory of the Left Front in 1977 was welcomed by large sections of the people. The circumstances were such that the Left's promise gave rise to both a feeling of relief and hope. These hopes were not belied, as several progressive measures taken by the Left government were exactly what the masses were looking for. These measures helped to change the power equations in the countryside in favour of the landless labourers, the share-croppers and the marginal farmers. In the process, however, the CPI(M) quickly gained domination over the Left Front. Over time, it was the perpetuation of that dominance that became the main objective, as the darker face of the ruling party, dizzy with success, began to appear.

In the initial years though it was sheer commitment that won minds and hearts for the Left. Economic adversities had paved the way for a sweeping anti-incumbency feeling. The worst famine of the century in 1943 had taken a toll of several million lives, with some estimates putting the figure at 3.5 million and others as high as 5 million or more. The 1950s were marked by a wave of agitations and protests. Beginning from a movement against increase of tram fares in 1953, protest movements on the issue of teachers salaries, against a ridiculous plan to merge Bengal and Bihar to solve the border problem between the two states and finally, on the demand for distribution of food at fair prices for the rural and urban poor rocked the state.

These movements were planned and carefully managed by the Left Front, a combination of Left parties in which the leading force was the undivided Communist Party of India (CPI). The bungled handling of these movements with the use of the undemocratic Security Act, which provided for detention without trial, had alienated the people and made the Congress government unpopular. Then in 1959 a procession of peasants from the rural areas—in which women with babies in arms had also participated—was brutally beaten up by the police, leading to a large number of deaths. Estimates of the toll vary; some put the figure as high as 80. The Congress was totally isolated, with many newspapers condemning the use of excessive force.

In 1953, the Calcutta Tramways Company, still a British company, decided to increase passenger fares by one paisa in both the classes. The first class fare was to go up from four paise to five and the second class from three to four paise. Even though this was a minuscule increase that in normal circumstances might have led only to a mild protest, it grew into a massive movement. The response to what was a minor change in fares burgeoned into a huge movement because of the context of unrest described earlier. It provided an opportunity to the huge population of discontented and frustrated people to give expression to their pent-up rage. The way this movement was handled by the home minister, Kalipada Mukherjee, further enraged the people.

There was a lathi charge at a rally called by the Left Front to protest against the fare increase, where not even the media was spared. Many reporters received injuries and, not unsurprisingly, the entire press came out with scathing editorials against the government's handling of the situation the next day. The government, which had fully supported the tramway company, appointed a committee to look into the matter of the fare increase, but this was only a face-saving device. It was clear that the fare increase would be withdrawn and it was.

Then came the teachers' movement. Teachers in West Bengal were being paid ridiculously low salaries, as little as an average annual salary of Rs 652 for lower primary schools and Rs 809 per annum for higher primary schools in 1955–56. Even the average salary of the college teachers was very low at Rs 3,070 per annum. With its repeated demands for a review of the scales being ignored, the All-Bengal Teachers Association (ABTA) gave a call for a strike. Large numbers of teachers squatted on the road right in front of the Esplanade junction.

With women in the majority, the teacher squatters attracted quite a lot of sympathy. Trade unions came with food packets to help them and the spot became a sort of pilgrimage centre. The teachers' demand being so legitimate, public sympathy was with them and public anger grew as the government refused to budge for days. Ultimately there was a midnight raid on the squatting teachers, and large-scale arrests took place. Once again, however, the government eventually yielded, and the Left steadily gained ground. I also got involved in the teachers' movement and addressed a number of teachers' meetings in north Calcutta. This was my first experience of the trade union movement. Later, I was actively associated with the Food Mazdoor Union led by the veteran trade union leader, Bishwanath Dubey.

Meanwhile, the attempt of the Congress government to muzzle the spiralling unrest over crippling food scarcity led to protests across West Bengal. The unbridled use of violence was matched by the militancy of the protests, which drew large segments of the people. On 31 August 1959, lakhs of people gathered at the Shaheed Minar to protest against food scarcity and rising prices. Among the thousands that had gathered were women with babies in arms. They had come because there was a state of semi-starvation among the poorer sections of the rural population—the landless labourers, the marginal farmers and rural artisans who had no work. They were squatting peacefully on the road leading to the East Gate of Raj Bhavan, quite a distance away from Writers' Building. According to reports then published, there was a brutal lathi charge that killed a large number, including women and children. Many more were injured.

The harsher the circumstances, the more militant was the protest of the people and the more severe the administrative backlash. The Congress regime's brutality ended up adding fuel to the fire as the food movement forged ahead even in the face of repression, gathering fresh momentum each day on scales that were unprecedented. Agitations erupted on many fronts, drawing in large segments of people. Demands for food security, release of political prisoners, higher salaries, dearness allowances of school-teachers under the secondary board of education and unemployment dole resonated throughout the state.

Between 1957 and 1962, West Bengal politics witnessed a sharp polarization: the ruling Congress found itself pitted against an increasingly formidable alliance of smaller Left parties under the leadership of the CPI. The popularity of the Left parties was on the rise but they were far behind the Congress in the electoral race, as was clear from the 1957 poll results. The Congress secured 152 seats against the Left's 46. There was, however, a dramatic about turn in the next five years when the Communist party, through militant movements, gained tremendously in credibility and popularity. Despite being charged with soft-pedaling China in the war against India, the CPI's vote share shot up from 18 per cent in 1957 to 25 per cent in 1962.

With no solution in sight to the food problem, apart from food imports from the United States under the PL 480 programme, and the growing unrest in West Bengal, a section of the Congress leadership came up with a ludicrous and extremely ill-advised strategy to check the surging tide of Left support in West Bengal. Upsetting the decision that had been taken by the States Reorganization Commission to set up states on linguistic lines, the Congress leadership of Bengal and Bihar proposed the merger of the two states in 1956. They thus hoped to douse the fires of revolt that were burning in West Bengal as, according to their political assessment, a combined state would have weakened the Communist movement. It was obvious that there would be no takers for it in West Bengal as the Bengalis would have become a minority in the joint state.

The plan announced with much fanfare aroused immediate opposition in West Bengal with the Left instantly calling for a total rejection of the plan and starting a satyagraha movement against the proposal. Just about this time, on 2 May 1956, there was a by-election for the Calcutta North West Parliamentary constituency. The Left opposition parties unanimously put up Mohit Moitra, a non-party left-leaning journalist and editor of a daily newspaper, as their candidate against the Congress. Moitra had been made convenor of the anti-merger campaign committee and the election was taken as a referendum on the merger proposal. A resounding victory for Mohit Moitra, defeating Ashok Kumar Sen of the Congress (who later on became the union law minister) by a huge margin of 33,073 votes, forced Bidhan Chandra Roy to make a statement withdrawing the merger proposal on 4 May 1956.

The writing on the wall was now clear. All these movements were leading to a groundswell of public opinion against the Congress government. The growing support for the Left was also reflected in the electoral results.

While all these movements were going on in West Bengal, events outside the state in Kerala and in the Soviet Union also exerted an influence on the political environment of the state.

Between the death of Stalin in March 1953 and the emergence of Khrushchev as the leader of the party in 1956, there had been a period of uncertainty in the Soviet Union. It was not clear whether Stalinist policies would continue or whether there would be a change. At the 20th Congress of the CPSU (Communist Party of the Soviet Union), however, along with Khrushchev's denunciation of Stalin, there was a major ideological shift with the acceptance of the possibility of a peaceful transition to socialism as against armed revolution, which had till then been considered the only way for a successful transition from capitalism to socialism. It was because of this that the Communists in India began to take the elections seriously and to entertain the idea that it would be possible and legitimate for the Communists to strive for and expect to come to power through elections.

The Kerala experience lent substance to that view. Events in Kerala between 1957 and 1959 had an impact on the Left and Communist movement in India as a whole but much more in West Bengal than elsewhere. Rather unexpectedly, in the second general election of the country in 1957, the Communist Party of India (CPI) in Kerala won nine seats in the Lok Sabha elections, against only six won by the Congress. In the Assembly elections held at the same time the Communists won 60 seats and, with the help of five independents, were able to get a majority—though a rather slender one in a house of 126.

For the first time anywhere in the world, the Communists were able to form a government through elections held under the Constitution of what the Communists themselves would consider to be a bourgeois democratic government. It was led by E.M.S. Namboodiripad, a popular leader who had taken part in the freedom movement and had founded the Congress Socialist Party in Kerala, which later converted itself into the Communist Party under his leadership. The Communist government soon ran into trouble, though. While the first of its measures, the Land Reform Ordinance followed by the Agrarian Reforms Bill was widely welcomed, its Educational Bill proved controversial and met with opposition, as it sought to curb the powers of church-led educational institutions as well as those of caste-led institutions such as the Nair Service Society.

An anti-Communist front was formed, which declared a 'liberation' war, putting pressure on the central government, which ultimately invoked Article 356 of the Constitution and dismissed the

Namboodiripad government. It is worth noting that the Congress president at this time was Indira Gandhi and it was at her insistence that Prime Minister Nehru, who was generally believed to be unenthusiastic about the measure, agreed to take the step. The dismissal of an elected government, which continued to have a majority in the Assembly, shocked people all over the country as it was felt to be a clear violation of democratic norms. That it happened while Nehru, who was known to have a soft corner for socialists, was the prime minister was even more galling for democratically-minded people.

In West Bengal in particular, where anti-Congress and even anti-Nehru feelings were strong, it helped to further strengthen the Communists. A huge protest demonstration, in which even sections of Congress supporters participated, marched through the streets of Calcutta. The bitterness of the confrontation between the Congress and the Left in West Bengal worsened after this action by the central government. State politics became sharply polarized between the Congress and the Left.

The present situation in India shows that the 'dead-letter' provision has, as B.R. Ambedkar hoped it would be, become a frequently invoked not-so-dead Article; it has been activated more than a hundred times till today. The National Commission to Review the Working of the Constitution (NCRWC), which was established on 22 February 2000, submitted its extensive report in March 2002. In its analysis, the NCRWC stated that in at least 20 out of the more than 100 instances, the invocation of Article 356 might be termed a misuse.

H.M. Seervai, the eminent jurist and former advocate-general of Maharashtra, who was offered a position as judge of the Supreme Court of India and declined, pointed out that only the President could remove the Governor and that the President acts on the advice of the Council of Ministers. Hence the Governor is in office effectively at the pleasure of the union executive. This may act as a bias whenever the Governor's duty requires him to go against the desires of the union executive. In its report, the NCRWC recommended that the President appoint or remove the chief minister in consultation with the Governor of the state.

Fali Nariman, MP (Rajya Sabha) and eminent jurist who was awarded Padma Bhushan in 1991, also rightly pointed out in an interview with a newspaper that the Constitution may not have envisaged a situation where an emergency arises in a state where the ruling party is of the same political persuasion as the one at the centre and that the centre might be biased against dissolving that government by invoking Article 356. He also pointed out that the word 'otherwise' in the text of Article 356 becomes instrumental in such a situation to allow the President to act without waiting for the Governor's report.

Between 1968 and 1977, President's Rule was imposed four times in West Bengal. P.C. Ghosh's PDF (Progressive Democratic Front) government, which was dismissed by Governor Dharam Vira in February 1968; Ajoy Mukherjee's United Front government in March 1970 and again his Democratic Front government in June 1971, which were dismissed by Governor S.S. Dhawan. Finally, in April 1977, governor A.L. Dias dismissed Siddhartha Sankar Ray's Congress government, on the view taken by the union government that the Congress's winning only three seats out of 42 seats in the Lok Sabha election implied a lack of confidence of the electorate in the government of the state.

In March 1959, the Dalai Lama left Tibet after Chinese troops shelled his palace and, travelling secretly, entered India. Tension between India and China had been building ever since Chinese forces occupied Tibet in 1950. The tension escalated after the Dalai

Lama crossed over into India and clashes between Chinese and Indian troops near the border took place on a number of occasions. Public opinion in India was inflamed when it was found out that the Chinese had built a road in Aksai Chin, which India considered to be within its territory.

The Communists refused to criticize the Chinese or to support the stand of the Indian government. This did not go down well with the people who considered that in supporting China because it was a Communist country and not siding with their own government, the Communists were taking an anti-national stand. The resentment against the Communists became particularly sharp after the Chinese launched a full-fledged invasion of India in October 1962. This led to a split in the Communist movement with one section under S.A. Dange condemning the Chinese aggression while another section continued to blame the Nehru government and refused to condemn the Chinese aggression.

The surge of the Left might have been arrested by an important development that took place in the late 1950s and early '60s but so deep was the alienation of the West Bengal masses from the Congress that, despite a brief setback, the Left movement was able to continue its onward journey.

The Party Splits; The Ultras Rise

Politics is not the art of the possible.
It consists in choosing between the disastrous and the unpalatable.

—John Kenneth Galbraith

In 1964, the united Communist Party fractured into the Communist Party of India and Communist Party of India (Marxist). At the root of the split were fundamental differences of perception regarding the character of the Indian state and its relations with the Congress. There was also a vital difference in their appraisals of the Chinese attack on India. One section, a majority in the undivided CPI, called it aggression. The other, minority, section refused to accept that a Communist state could ever be the aggressor. It blamed the Indian government for having provoked the Chinese.

Thus were the seeds of the 1964 split sown in 1962 at a National Council meeting held in Delhi. The party was all but divided when the CPI leader and veteran Communist leader S.A. Dange proposed a resolution condemning the aggression that was passed by a majority of the delegates, but one-third of the number walked out, refusing to support the resolution. It was that group that later met in 1964 and formed the CPI(M): the Communist Party of India (Marxist).

S.A. Dange considered the Congress to be a party of the national bourgeoisie and supported co-operation with it, while the CPI(M) believed that the Congress represented the interests of landlords and the bourgeoisie and preferred a policy of confrontation with and opposition to the Congress. The increasing differences between the CPSU (Communist Party of the Soviet Union) and the CPC (Communist Party of China) widened the rift in the undivided Communist Party of India.

While Bhupesh Gupta, Indrajit Gupta, Somnath Lahiri and Bishwanath Mukherjee remained with the CPI, the other top leaders Jyoti Basu, Pramode Dasgupta, Harekrishna Konar and Saroj Mukherjee joined the CPI(M). It is said that Jyoti Basu was undecided till the last minute about throwing in his lot with the CPI(M). He was more in line with the CPI regarding its tactical approach of aligning with the Congress to strengthen socialist forces in the country and also to expand the reach and the base of the Communist movement.

In more ways than one, 1967 was a watershed in West Bengal's politics. The first United Front government headed by Ajoy Mukherjee ascended to power, ushering in a period of protracted instability, shaky governments collapsing on top of each other, chief ministers entering and exiting in the blink of an eye and the threat of President's Rule hanging like a noose about to tighten its grip. At the outset, when the coalition took charge, hope was renewed. The CPI(M) was poised on the threshold of a new political beginning, when yet another debate over participation in the United Front government began to rage within the party over joining the United Front government, with Jyoti Basu and Pramode Dasgupta holding tangentially opposite views.

Interestingly, even in 1967 Jyoti Basu was in favour of participating in the United Front government and was successful in carrying the party along with him. It is not without irony that three decades down the line, in the middle of 1996, a similar debate in the CPI(M) resulted in the historic blunder of not permitting Jyoti Basu to become the first Communist prime minister of India.

Pramode Dasgupta provided leadership to the group known then as 'Leftists' and later as 'hardliners', who opposed participation. Unlike in 1996, Basu at that time could carry the party with him. At the end of an intense debate, the CPI(M) decided to join the coalition, which elected Basu as its deputy chief minister. The United Front government had an ambitious agenda with an eighteen-point programme committed to improving food supply, creating more jobs and better health facilities. More importantly, it laid the ground for an uninterrupted, thirty four-year-long Left Front rule in the state from 1977. That was still a few years away, though.

With the Congress divided and in disarray and the Communists leading popular protests one after another, the Left parties were on a roll. The formation of the first United Front government in 1967 with the participation of the CPI(M) justified Jyoti Basu's strategy and line of thinking. The mid-term election of 1969 projected a bi-polar contest between the United Front and the Congress, with the Front securing 214 seats and the Congress only 55 seats. The CPI(M), with 80 seats, emerged as the single largest party in the West Bengal Assembly for the first time. By 1967-69, Chinese aggression was no more an emotional issue. CPI(M)'s gain was largely because of split of Congress both at National and State levels. The unpopularity of the Congress was at its peak and during the split between CPM and CPI, most of rank and file preferred to join the CPM. The CPI, as it did not join the United Left Front with CPM in 1967 preferring PULF—Peoples United Left Front led by Bangla Congress, the CPM emerged as the main anti-Congress force, thus electorally benefiting in a big way. However, Ajoy Mukherjee of the Bangla Congress, despite securing fewer seats, got the position of chief minister, denying the CPI(M)'s Jyoti Basu his due position. It was obvious though that the scales were tipping in favour of the Left.

However, a new path opened up before the CPI(M) as the party was put in charge of critical portfolios like land and land revenue, labour, relief and rehabilitation and transport. Basu's argument for his party's tactical participation in government was bearing fruit. Working overtime, the CPI(M) started building its profile among the people, expanding its support base.

Harekrishna Konar, land and land revenue minister, tackled the distribution of *benami* land, that is, land registered in the name of a proxy owner, on a war footing. Of the 32 points on the government's charter of commitments, land distribution was perhaps the most successful, the most talked-about programme. This was a critical journey in the political life of the CPI(M) and, in many ways, a precursor to 1977, the turning point in the party's destiny.

In the 13 months that the government survived, the CPI(M) created new aspirations among the landless underclass, disturbing entrenched power relations in the countryside. Bengal continued to be in turmoil: industrial unrest was escalating; *gheraos* were becoming routine, the political landscape in villages was changing beyond recognition; Naxalbari was born, as armed radicals killed and got killed. Without doubt the defining phase of this period lay in Naxalbari, in the armed insurrection of its peasants.

The rivalry between the Congress and the CPI(M), however, occupied considerable public space as the Communists rapidly gained ground, especially in rural Bengal over the 1960s and '70s, while the Congress was bent on destroying them. The Communists not only survived but went from strength to strength, finally ascending to power in 1977. Who would have imagined such a stunning change in the political equation? Who would have believed the 'party of struggle' would be in the seat of governance for the next three decades? In the years and decades to come, compulsions of governance would increasingly collide with the politics of militant struggle. In the process, it would make the 'revolutionary' party an expert at doublespeak. Meanwhile, the Naxal movement was assuming menacing proportions.

Three years after the Communist Party split, political restlessness engulfed the CPI(M) as Naxalbari came to life, shifting the course of the Indian Communist movement once more. Inspired by Mao Zedong's historic slogan 'Power flows from the barrel of the gun', armed insurrectionists ignited the first flame of rebellion in Naxalbari, a little-known area of Siliguri.

Charu Mazumdar, the founder of the Naxal movement had, with his comrades, been active in organizing Siliguri's tea estate workers since 1954. As the CPI formed the Siliguri Krishak Sabha in 1959 for recovering *benami* land, Mazumdar intensified his activities in the Naxalbari area. In 1967, the CPI(M) organized a convention of peasants in Siliguri, urging them to form committees and seize *benami* land. Kanu Sanyal, a leading Naxal leader, was then part of the CPI(M)'s Krishak Samiti. The ground was being laid for an ideological and programmatic conflict within the CPI(M), which eventually split the party.

As the peasant movement grew formidable, the United Front government launched a no-holds-barred repression. In retaliation to the killing of one policeman, security forces on 25 May laid siege to a village, killing nine persons, including six women and two children. In retrospect, the similarity between what happened more than forty years later in Nandigram is striking.

Within the CPI(M), increasing dissension led to the formation of the All-India Coordination Committee of Revolutionaries (AICCR), which declared that peoples' democratic revolution could only be achieved by overthrowing 'U.S. imperialism, Soviet revisionism, Indian landlords and comprador bourgeoisie'. Harekrishna Konar attempted reconciliation with the militant peasants in vain. Mazumdar urged them to jettison the CPI(M)'s 'class collaborationist and revisionist' ideology.

The Naxal movement was a ruthless expression of revolutionary violence, which provoked unprecedented brutal retaliation by the state. Inspired and romanticized by the revolutionary thoughts of Mao Tse-Tung and Lenin who advocated, 'It is necessary to create a terror for a while to over throw the authority' (*Selected Works of Mao*) and that 'the proletariat needs state power, the Centralized organization of force, the organization of violence for the purpose of guiding the great mass of population—the peasantry, the petite bourgeoisie, the semi-proletarians—in the work of organizing socialist economy (V.I. Lenin, *State and Revolution*). Many idealist youths joined Naxalbari movement to overthrow the government. Fear did not shackle young, idealistic minds. Thousands of middle-class students quit educational institutions and jettisoned prospects of bright careers to join the militant struggle. Giving up the charmed circles of elite colleges, students went to live in the depths of a poverty-ridden countryside.

It was not destined to succeed but despite its cold-bloodedness the movement was haunted by a certain romantic innocence, with its messianic spirit of a political crusade against exploitation and injustice. Naxalism, interchangeably referred to as Naxals or Maoists continues to inspire many people to lead to an armed revolution, even now.

The Naxal period was a difficult time, particularly for the youth in Bengal. I lived in Sobhabazar in north Calcutta, a place not considered very safe on account of my journalistic and political commitments. It was a known den of Naxals—even a Congress MLA, Nepal Roy, was shot dead in broad day light in this area. It was often scary to return home late at night but I was never touched. Indeed, the neighbourhood boys would protect me: '*Dada ektu poray jaben*' (Brother, please leave a little later). Sometimes they would guide me: '*Paasher goli diyay cholay jaan*' (Take the side lane). The Naxals then were idealists and never harmed anyone other than their 'class' enemies. Later, however, there emerged all kind of Naxals: police Naxals, real Naxals, fake Naxals and more. Those were the days when the police took a policy decision to eliminate naxalities by killing them, even resorting to fake counters killing many innocent youth. I was more afraid of the police, who were on a killing spree.

As a journalist, I came into the contact with Ranjit Gupta, the last member of the Indian Police to become Calcutta's commissioner of police (CP) and later on inspector-general of police (IGP). He issued me an identity card, signing it himself, to 'save me from the police'. He did not forget to warn me that if the Naxals found the card with me, only God could save me. Ranjit Gupta was a brilliant officer, very knowledgeable, who would occasionally write anonymously in *The Statesman* on varied subjects. However, he courted many controversies and faced severe criticism for his role during the Naxal period, since he was considered to have masterminded the division among the naxalities, as well as the fake encounters that ultimately ended up eliminating them.

Both the United Front and, subsequently, the Congress government had to grapple with the Naxal insurgency and failed to stem the tide of violence. The police were given far-reaching powers, including that of arresting without warrant, with the passage of the West Bengal Prevention of Violent Activities Bill in 1970. Instead of looking for political, social or economic solutions, the government opted for the 'police solution' of physically eliminating Naxalites. Hundreds of suspected Naxals were just shot dead. In my presence at his residence, the redoubtable police commissioner once demanded of the officer-in-charge of Jorabagan Police Station, '*Aami mundu chai*' (I want heads).

Several disturbing developments took place on 30 March 1971. I had gone to Ranjit Gupta's home to get a story. He was not in a good mood, very irritable and disturbed. He came out of his house and, looking at his guards, reprimanded them for their shabby dress and unacceptable lack of physical fitness. Gupta then asked me to get into his car. Sensing his disturbed frame of mind, I just hopped in, hoping that he would talk to me enroute to work. Apart from mentioning that he would go to the medical college to pay homage to a killed constable on his way to the police headquarters at Lal Bazar, he was absolutely silent, apparently in deep thought.

Suddenly he started talking, as if to himself, 'There is no other way out. I do not know. I only hope peace returns to Bengal. My hair is graying fast. I have started horse riding again. My horse is putting on weight but I am losing weight.' Before I could interject, the wireless in his car came alive. There were frantic messages to and fro with the CP issuing instructions into the phone. In between, he instructed his driver to go to B.K. Paul Avenue. Obviously, he had changed his mind about visiting the medical college. I mumbled that I would get off near the office of *The Statesman*, on the way.

His instructions were now louder and more specific. I realized that Congress leader Nepal Roy had been shot dead and the CP was going directly to the spot: Nepal Roy's office on B.K. Paul Avenue. He was understandably very tense. I wanted to get off because it was not considered wise to be seen with the police and there would be a lot of people, including the media at the spot, which was also my *paara* (neighbourhood). I was wondering how to ask him to drop me off when he suddenly asked his driver to stop the car, near the Central Avenue Coffee House. He said, '*Aaray aapnar kothaye nambar chhilo?*' (Oh where was I supposed to drop you?) I do not remember what I said but I just ran out of the car, entered the Coffee House and ordered toast and hot coffee as I tried to regain my composure.

When I reached home at night, my parents were very disturbed over the murder in our neighbourhood. Nepal Roy's office was a few yards away from my house. I was rebuked and warned that the door would not be opened for me if I came home after dusk. They knew that I would not listen. The *paara* boys excitedly told me that the CP had arrived within minutes of the murder; even before the DC (deputy commissioner) and OC (officer-in-charge) and he reprimanded them publicly. I acted the part of a curious listener.

I had actively participated in the Assembly elections of 1967 and 1969. This was the period of my political association with the Forward Bloc. I closely observed the functioning of the United Front governments and was witness to many happenings both at Writers' Building and the Assembly House. In 1967, two fronts, the United Left Front (ULF) led by the CPI(M) and the Peoples' United Left Front (PULF) led by the Bangla Congress fought the elections against the Congress. I was close to the PULF, comprising the Bangla Congress, the CPI and the Forward Bloc. During this period I developed a good rapport with many leaders such as Ajoy Mukherjee, Ashok Ghosh, Somnath Lahiri, Hemanta Kumar Basu, Biswanath Mukherjee and Sushil Dhara, among others.

I have many memories of these selfless leaders. They were simple and honest men with a mission and commitment, unlike many of today's leaders. They inspired me. Ajoy Mukherjee and Hemanta Basu were unbelievably innocent in many ways. Hemanta Babu was the public works and housing minister. His chamber in Writers' Building was open to one and all, no one was refused a meeting, and requests were rarely turned down. As a result, he would often allot a government flat to more than one applicant. I recall one of his officers coming to him to seek his final approval to settle such cases, when I was with him. Hemanta Babu asked me to sit with his officers to scrutinize the applications with the advice, 'Ensure that no one is deprived.' Hemanta Babu was very upset that there were not enough government flats to satisfy all the needy people. I was deeply shocked and grieved when he was shot dead, allegedly by the Naxals.

By 1969, most Left parties had come under the single banner of the United Front but all its constituent parties vigorously protected their constituencies, even at the expense of inter-party feuds and violence. I remember travelling with the Forward Bloc Marxist leader Ram Chatterjee in the districts. While addressing his supporters he cajoled them to strengthen the party, even suggesting that they crush the other parties. When one local leader pointed out that they were a part of the United Front, Ram Chatterjee declared loudly, '*Bhotere shomoy jukto front, Ekhun shudhu party.*' (United Front only during elections; now only our party.)

The CPI(M) made the best use of critical portfolios like home, land and land revenue, labour, relief and rehabilitation and transport. In the 13 months during which the government survived, the CPI(M) laid the foundation for its return to power in 1977. It created new aspirations among the landless and changed the class power structure in the villages, with Harekrishna Konar as land and land revenue minister working overtime to distribute *benami* land. For the first time, the labouring sections, with the means of *gherao* at their disposal, felt emboldened and protected. Jyoti Basu's tactical line was yielding results in terms of expanding the Left's support base.

My memory goes back to 1962 when, as a teenager, I had participated in a procession to protest against the Chinese invasion of India. I remember lending my voice to the protesters screaming: 'Down with China'; 'Down with the Communists' without fully understanding what or why I was doing so. It was the tri-colour that fluttered in West Bengal and in the whole country at that time and any other position seemed to be unpatriotic to us. Much later, after a lapse of 24 years, I was somehow instrumental in contributing to easing of tension between India and China during the 1986 Sino-India border skirmishes.

It was during my visit to China as the Deputy Leader of the goodwill delegation of the Indian Federation of United Nations Associations (Ifuna), in 1987 on the invitation of United Nations Associations of China. The visit that was considered a simple bilateral goodwill visit turned out to be politically and even strategically very significant.

While flying within China on a Chinese Airlines flight, I chanced upon a government of China's English publication. The cover story startled me. It talked about border skirmishes alleging incursions by the Indian Army and forcible occupation of some advanced posts in the Sumdorong Chu valley area that, according to Chinese, were in their territory. The news was threatening and warned of grave consequences for India.

A very high level meeting with Liu Shuqing, Vice Foreign Minister of China was scheduled during our visit. On the morning of our scheduled meeting, I got a phone call from Shiv Shankar Menon from the Indian Embassy in China expressing his desire to meet me. Politely declining to come to my room, he wanted me to come down and took me out for a stroll.

Quickly coming to the point. Menon said: 'I understand you are meeting Liu Shuqing and that you will be leading the discussion'. He said that as far as the India-China border talks were concerned, this Chinese Vice Foreign Minister was very important, as he was the leader of the Chinese delegation for the border talks. There were some problems on the border, Menon said. I told him what I had read in a Chinese publication and he confirmed, simply saying: 'Yes, there are some developments' and gave me the Indian version of the incident.

He came to the main point. It was China's turn to visit India for the border talks, and the Chinese were stalling it on one pretext or the other. Without my realizing it, Menon had given me a three-fold assignment: first explain the Indian position vis-à-vis the border skirmishes, stating firmly that the government of India had no intention to escalate the dispute. Second, figure out what the Chinese had to say about the incidents and how strongly they felt about it. Third and most importantly, why were the Chinese stalling the next round of talks and when did they propose to visit India for this purpose. Menon, then a counsellor in the Indian Embassy, rose to become foreign secretary of India and the national security advisor.

The ever-smiling Chinese Liu Shuqing was polite but firm and forceful. Although he knew English, he used an interpreter. Being a seasoned and shrewd diplomat his replies were mostly general and vague in nature and full of platitudes. I finally managed to provoke him by accusing China of disturbing the peace at the border.

'Indian troops have recently trespassed into Chinese territory at Wang Dong and are almost face to face with the Chinese Army—only a dozen metres away from each other. It is very dangerous. The troops must withdraw, otherwise some serious problem will arise,' the Chinese vice foreign minister warned. His tone had the familiar ring of 1962. Menon later rejected the claim to me saying 'We have been at Wang Dong for years together. There is no trespass. We are in our territory.' When asked if the good relations between India and the Soviet Union stood in the way of better Sino-Indian relations the vice foreign minister remarked wryly, 'We do not know what was in the minds of Indian leaders at that time and why the border dispute was created.' He added 'Nehru was taken in by the Soviet Leader, Khrushchev, and the 1962 conflict came about.' Mr Liu considered as Soviet expert had worked as Political Counsellor at the Chinese Embassy in the Soviet Union. The Chinese diplomat also hinted at external pressure for a hardening of the Indian stance.

The Chinese leader was not forthcoming on the next date for the border talks despite my proddings. The last round was held in Beijing in July 1986 and it is now the turn of New Delhi to host the next. But as the custom goes it is the guest who suggests the date to the host, and New Delhi is waiting for Beijing to do so. Liu smiled and said, 'It is now hot in New Delhi. May be sometime in cooler weather, we can meet for border talks.' Obviously, he was hinting at the heat generated by the present tension on the border. I persisted, 'Your Excellency, are you referring to political climate, otherwise it is not so hot.' That got him laughing and he closed the meeting with an assuring and smiling response, 'We will meet soon.'

Shiv Shankar Menon, who was waiting for me to return at the hotel lobby, did not even allow me to go to my room. While walking in the garden, I briefed him. He was intently noting down, each word, repeating it to confirm that he had got it right. He thanked me profusely and rushed back, possibly to dispatch a cable to his bosses in New Delhi. Considering the volatile situation on the Sino-India border and the importance of the discussion on my return, I sent a long and detailed note about my meeting through the then cabinet minister Ram Niwas Mirdha, to the then Prime Minister

Rajiv Gandhi. There was an immediate response inviting me to Delhi to brief senior Ministry of External Affairs officials. Later, based on my interview, I wrote articles in *The Statesman* (edition of 20 July 1987) and in the Onlooker, an English magazine published from Bombay.

Both India and China had realized the danger of an inadvertent conflict and, after initial posturing, the decision was made to de-escalate their deployments. India's Foreign Minister, N.D. Tiwari, visited Beijing in May 1987 and the first formal flag meeting to discuss 'the freezing of the situation' since 1962 was held in August 1987. In the following year, Prime Minister Rajiv Gandhi made his historic visit to Beijing. The rest is the history.

The Turbulent Years

I am sometimes a fox and sometimes a lion.
The whole secret of government lies in knowing when to be the one or the other.

—Napolean Bonaparte

After Independence, Mahatma Gandhi had declared Jawaharlal Nehru as his heir and Nehru took charge as the prime minister. He was what, in political parlance, has been described as left of centre. There were, however, from the beginning, forces in the Cabinet that could be described as right of centre. Sardar Vallabhbhai Patel, the home minister, represented this school. After Patel's death in 1950, Nehru dominated the government and the party but there were right-wing forces that were active both within the Congress and outside. In successive elections in 1952, 1957 and 1962 the Congress party won a majority under Nehru's leadership.

The Chinese attack in October 1962 dealt a severe blow to Pandit Nehru personally as he was seen as having totally misread the Chinese leaders and succumbed to the charms of Chou En Lai, who proved to be a superior diplomat. The Chinese premier had extracted support for China's sovereignty over Tibet without giving anything in return to Nehru in the form of either a well-defined border or an acknowledgement of India's claim to Kashmir. It was an even more serious blow to the left-leaning elements within the Congress who were under attack from the right-wing elements.

V.K. Krishna Menon, the defence minister, had to resign in the face of pressure from the right wing within Parliament and outside. After the passing of Jawaharlal Nehru, the right-wing forces tried to dominate the Congress and the election of the prime minister, which had been unanimous as long as Nehru was alive, began to be a source of contention between right and left forces, within and outside Parliament.

It was at this juncture that my modest participation in the political developments began. It was the left end of the political spectrum that attracted me. Just out of school and still in my teens, I came into contact with a Calcutta-based organization called the Study Group. It described itself as a group of the city's progressive intellectuals and regularly organized seminars and discussions on important issues facing society and the nation. Its leader had migrated to Calcutta in 1954 from Bihar, where he had come into contact with the Communist Party of India, which was quite a strong force in the state at that time.

Fourteen years my senior, his socialist and progressive views moulded my thinking at that impressionable age. Our group ventured into journalism and brought out a Hindi fortnightly, *Vichar Pravah,* with serious articles tilted towards socialist ideology. I was appointed assistant editor and my main task was to translate English articles into Hindi. Some of the articles given to me were from the information department of the Consulate-General of the Soviet Union in Calcutta. I found them very interesting and exciting. An article about the differences between the Soviet and the Chinese Communist Parties was published in our fortnightly in 1964. It was slightly tilted towards the Chinese ideological stance. That was why, I suppose, at one of the diplomatic cocktail parties a Soviet diplomat, who had evidently been told about that article, cornered me and gave me a long harangue on the situation in the international Communist movement.

I was thrilled that I had received recognition as a journalist and that my article had attracted attention. We had also established contact with and even come close to such progressive Congress leaders as V.K. Krishna Menon and K.D. Malaviya. It was during the 68th session of Congress at Bhubaneswar in January 1964 that K.D. Malaviya thought that socialist forces within the Congress should be strengthened, and proposed that a force of 1,000 progressive youths, committed to democratic socialism, be organized in the country to strengthen socialist ideas.

He came to Calcutta to interview and select such youths and met me amongst others for a personal interview. He asked, 'Why do you believe in socialism?' and all that I could say was, 'Because my leader believes in it.' I was only about eighteen years old, and naïve. Perhaps my apparent honesty and sincerity got me selected. However, I did not hear much about this thereafter. The idea had petered out.

Our quest to strengthen socialist forces within the Congress led us to be actively associated with the Congress Forum for Socialist Action, a forum within the Congress promoted by progressive Congressmen under the patronage of Gulzari Lal Nanda, who was then home minister of India. After Nehru's death, Lal Bahadur Shastri and Nanda had come together against the Syndicate, a loose body of right-wing Congressmen. Prominent among them were Atulya Ghosh, Neelam Sanjiva Reddy, Morarji Desai and S.K. Patil, who were critical of Nehru during his last years as prime minister. The Congress Forum brought our group close to Nanda. In the inner-Congress factional divide at that time, the Atulya Ghosh group represented the right wing and the Ajoy Mukherjee group the other side. We were with Ajoy Mukherjee. At a Congress workers' convention in Calcutta, Atulya Ghosh publicly accused Nanda, in his presence, of organizing and supporting people to oppose him in Bengal, referring, of course, to our group.

The conflicts at the centre had clearly infected the Congress at the provincial level in West Bengal. Atulya Ghosh and Ajoy Mukherjee, top state leaders, were in the thick of a brinkmanship battle, which eventually led to their parting ways in 1965. Expelled by his party, Ajoy Mukherjee floated a new outfit, the Bangla Congress. This was also when the Communist party was tossing and turning in an intra-party ideological conflict, which finally forced a split. My association with the Bangla Congress and Ajoy Mukherjee started at this time.

Earlier, in November 1964, we had organized a Congress socialist workers' convention in Calcutta inviting some Young Turks, including Bhagwat Jha Azad, Amarnath Vidyalankar, Harshdeo Malaviya, Arjun Arora, Shashi Bhushan and others. I remember an interesting incident. They were staying in a very modest accommodation in Central Calcutta, sharing rooms with twin beds. One morning Bhagwat Jha Azad said, 'You should never put two socialists in a room. By the morning they will set up a third party. Also, if two "rightists" stay together they will develop a united enterprise.' It was a sad comment on the divisive state of affairs among the socialist forces in the country.

The rift between the factions within the Congress was so deep that our group began receiving threatening calls from the Atulya Ghosh camp and we were forced to seek protection from the union home minister, Gulzari Lal Nanda, who deputed Shanti Kothari, an officer on special duty in the home ministry, to oversee arrangements for our protection. Shanti Kothari later became a member of the Rajya Sabha. Also, a delegation of the Congress Forum for Socialist Action was invited by the home minister to meet Prime Minister Shastri in New Delhi. Deepankar Ghosh, senior political correspondent, covered this piece of news prominently in *The Statesman*. However, before the meeting could take place, Shastri died on 10 January 1966 while in Moscow where he was discussing ceasefire terms with the

Pakistani President Ayub Khan, mediated by the Soviet leaders.

Several meetings took place in the office of the Study Group at Sudhir Chatterjee Street in north Calcutta in connection with the formation of the Bangla Congress. At one of these meetings, the draft of the constitution of the Bangla Congress was being discussed in the presence of Ajoy Mukherjee, Sushil Dhara and others. The draft was not considered very satisfactory and I remember commenting, 'There is hardly any content except hereby and thereby.' I was promptly included in the group that was asked to brush it up.

It was a natural process of indoctrination. I now believed in socialism and was pleased to consider myself a progressive. I used to read the *Patriot*, an English daily, *Link*, the magazine with socialistic pro-Soviet views published from Delhi and *Blitz*, run by the well-known pro-Soviet journalist R.K. Karanjia. I remember sending a letter to the editor of *Blitz* decrying the efforts of the rightists in the Congress to dilute the resolution on socialism.

My letter to the editor was published in the 'People's Parliament Column' of *Blitz* of 22 October 1966 under the caption 'Duplicity of Congress'. It read 'You rightly deserve congratulations for exposing the tactics of cheating the people through "magic of words" in the Congress Election Manifesto. Not only will both the wings of Congress interpret it in their own way, the leaders will also place two meanings on the term "Social Control On Banks". On the one hand, they will convince voters it is a step towards the nationalization of banks and, on the other hand, they will collect "Election Fund", placing this term before "Money Bags" as a guarantee of no-nationalization of banks.' I was then twenty years old.

In the fourth general election to the West Bengal Assembly in 1967, a People's United Left Front was formed, led by Ajoy Mukherjee, leader of the Bangla Congress and supported by the CPI and Forward Bloc. This was the first general election of my adult life and I had the chance to participate fully and actively, and not just as a voter. We fielded the leader of our group as a Forward Bloc candidate from the Jorasanko constituency in north Calcutta. Our candidate lost but the whole experience served as a kind of political apprenticeship for me.

In the triangular fight between the Congress, the ULF led by the CPI(M) and the PULF, led by the Bangla Congress and the CPI, the Congress, with 127 seats, lost its majority for the first time since independence in West Bengal. During the 1967 elections, I came close to Forward Bloc leaders, particularly its powerful general secretary Ashok Ghosh, with whom I still have good relations. His understanding of politics, easy accessibility and down-to-earth approach impressed me.

To return to the chronological sequence of events leading to the decline of Congress and the resultant rise of the Left in West Bengal, after the 1967 Assembly elections, the opposition groups (ULF and PULF) were merged as the United Front (UF) and the first non-Congress United Front government was formed with an ex-Congressman, Ajoy Kumar Mukherjee, who had won from two constituencies, as chief minister and Jyoti Basu as his deputy.

The UF government that took oath on 2 March 1967, survived for only 263 days, collapsing on 20 November 1967. Trust was a major issue and even after the 1967 elections, the CPI(M), despite being the largest party in the United Front with 43 seats, was not given the post of chief minister. The Bangla Congress's distrust of the Left was so deep that even the home ministry was denied to Jyoti Basu, who became the deputy chief minister in charge of the finance and home (transport) departments. With no party or front securing a majority, a coalition government seemed inevitable.

On 2 December 1967, the state food and agriculture minister, P.C. Ghosh, resigned and withdrew his support from the Ajoy Mukherjee government, along with 17 other members of the Assembly. P.C. Ghosh and his colleagues formed a new parliamentary party, the Progressive Democratic Front (PDF) and staked claim before Governor Dharam Vira to form the government. The leader of the Congress party also announced his party's support for Ghosh. The Governor requested the chief minister to call the Assembly into session as early as possible and not later than the third week of November 1967 on the grounds that doubts had been raised about the support of the majority of the members of the Assembly for the United Front government led by Ajoy Mukherjee.

The cabinet did not accept the Governor's request as it had already decided to call the Assembly into session on 18 December 1967. The Governor rejected the contention of the council of ministers and, on 21 November, issued an order under Article 164(1) of the Constitution of India dismissing Ajoy Mukherjee's government, and invited the PDF headed by P.C. Ghosh to form the new government. As the stalemate continued due to deadlock created by the Speaker, President's Rule was imposed on 20 February 1968.

There was a huge rally at the Maidan organized by the United Front to protest the dissolution of the Ajoy Mukherjee government. Bejoy Kumar Banerjee, Speaker of the West Bengal Legislative Assembly was the hero of the crowd. I was present at this rally. Bejoy Banerjee dramatically displayed a key, saying that the Assembly was locked and the key was with him. 'Exercising power vested in me under Rule 15 of the procedure of the Assembly, I have adjourned the house *sine die* on the grounds that the dissolution of the United Front ministry, the appointment of Dr P.C. Ghosh as chief minister and the summoning of the House on Dr Ghosh's advice were unconstitutional and invalid as they had been affected behind the back of the house,' Bejoy Kumar Banerjee announced. The crowd was jubilant.

West Bengal politics, however, was in a state of turmoil. The mid-term election of 1969 in West Bengal resulted in a decisive victory for the United Front. The CPI(M) with 80 seats emerged as the largest party. The strength of the Congress was drastically reduced from 127 in 1967 to a mere 55 in 1969. The second United Front government, with Ajoy Mukherjee as chief minister, took office on 25 February 1969. This time the CPI(M), which had gained considerable strength, demanded and got the home department with general administration and police being given to Jyoti Basu as deputy chief minister.

Soon, however, differences arose between the CPI(M) and the Bangla Congress and once again the U F government was threatened with dissolution and imposition of President's Rule. There was furore all over the country against the political machinations of the Congress led Central government, to dismiss the United Front government, which was supported by industrialists. My friends and I, then at the helm of the *Blitz* National Forum, a reader's forum of *Blitz* National Weekly, in West Bengal, organized a massive public meeting with the cry, 'Save the UF Government' at Subodh Mullick Square in central Calcutta.

The editor of *Blitz*, R.K. Karanjia, flew from Bombay on our invitation to preside over the meeting on 25 January 1970. Ajoy Mukherjee came straight from the United Front reconciliation meeting, which he described as the 'Supreme Court of the People' to break the news that the Front had been saved. CPI leader Indrajit Gupta also addressed the meeting, endorsing the chief minister's assurances.

Russi Karanjia had, of course, held separate meetings with Ajoy Mukherjee and Jyoti Basu. Even senior Congress leader V.K. Krishna Menon intervened to ensure a peaceful resolution of the differences within the constituents of the United Front. Earlier, Russi Karanjia addressed a meeting and press conference at the Calcutta Press Club organized by the Hindi weekly *Jan Sansar*, of which I was the assistant editor and which was presided over by Vivekananda Mukherjee, the doyen of Bengal journalists and the editor of *Basumati*. The meeting was covered by the *Blitz* issue of 31 January 1970.

However, this patched-up Front did not survive for long, and Ajoy Mukherjee resigned as chief minister on 19 March 1971. Jyoti Basu's claim to form the government was not accepted by the Governor and most parties were opposed to a government led by the CPI(M). As a result, disparate groups got together and a democratic coalition government led by Ajoy Kumar Mukherjee of the Bangla Congress and with Bijoy Singh Nahar of the Congress(R) as deputy chief minister was formed on 2 April 1971. The other, smaller, parties, including the SSP, PSP, Gorkha League and Muslim League also joined the government. The CPI, FB and Congress(O) also supported the government from the outside but it survived for two months only, following a split in the Bangla Congress.

During 1970-71, the state went under President's Rule twice. First, following the resignation of Ajoy Mukherjee as chief minister of the United Front government. On 16 March 1970, Governor Shanti Swarup Dhawan came to the conclusion that there was no prospect of an alternative ministry and recommended President's Rule. After the elections, Ajoy Mukherjee of the Bangla Congress as the leader of the Democratic Front, who enjoyed a thin majority, advised the Governor to dissolve the Assembly and tendered his resignation on 28 June 1971. President's Rule was imposed the next day and continued till March 1972.

Amidst this extremely fluid political situation, in November 1969, the Congress split in two. In the 1971 mid-term election its two factions contested against each other. With the dissolution of the Assembly on 25 June 1971 the stage was set for fresh elections in 1972. Bengal politics was wracked by violence; divisions, mergers, and new alliances were the order of the day. Then came the murder of Hemanta Basu and the election in Shyampukur constituency was countermanded. The by-election in that constituency was also countermanded following the murder of another FB candidate, Ajit Biswas. So were the elections in Uktra and Dum Dum because of more candidates being murdered, allegedly by Naxalites. Violence was at its peak in 1971.

The 1972 Assembly election, which took place in such a charged atmosphere, also became hugely controversial. The CPI(M) and other allied parties raised complaints of colossal rigging and corrupt practices by the Congress. As a result, the CPI(M), the WPI (Workers Party of India) and the SUCI (Socialist Unity Centre of India, a state level recognized political party) boycotted the Assembly and called Siddhartha Sankar Ray's government an illegal one. The Congress secured a massive 216 seats out of 280 and formed its first government after five years. The Bangla Congress had split into two with the Bangla Congress (Ajoy Mukherjee) merging with the Congress and the Bangla Congress (Sushil Dhara) joining hands with the Congress (O). In an allegedly rigged election, the tally of the CPI(M) came down to 14 seats. What also had an impact at the local level was the great Bangladesh victory under the leadership of Indira Gandhi. This was a triumph for the Congress and led to its thumping victory in the 1971 Lok Sabha polls. It won 351 seats out of 518, securing 43.60 per cent of the votes.

From October 1962, when the Chinese attacked India, the Congress had been steadily losing support in West Bengal. By the end of the decade and after the dismissal of two non-Congress governments its isolation was all but complete. The Left had already tasted power through two stints in office, albeit in coalition governments led by the leader of a breakaway group of the Congress, and which had ended abruptly with the draconian Article 356 being invoked. That the Left was gradually inching forward was becoming clear and it was apparent that sooner or later a Left government without the encumbrance of sharing power with splinter groups of the Congress would emerge. However, the war with Pakistan in 1971 delayed this prospect a little.

Power or no power, there were problems galore for the CPI(M). Come 1969, it was time for another split and a more sinister one at that. Within the CPI(M) increased dissension led to the formation in April 1969, the birth centenary of Lenin, of (CPI-ML)—Communist Party of India (Marxist-Leninist)—that split from CPI(M). Then followed a period of unprecedented lawlessness, violence and terror, marked by Naxals attacking and killing those they considered enemies of the people. On the other side there was brutal repression by the state. Calcutta slid into a bottomless pit of fear.

One instance comes to my mind. On 29 July 1969 a policeman was killed at Basanti in South 24 Parganas in a clash with SUC supporters. Two days later, on 31 July, a group of policemen suddenly entered the Assembly premises with the body of their colleague and began to vandalize property. The crowd entered the chamber of Home Minister Jyoti Basu, shouting, 'Down with the UF government.' The government dismissed the thirteen policemen but times were clearly turbulent in West Bengal.

As a youth in Calcutta in the late 1960s and early 1970s, I came into contact with Naxals, who seemed to me to be young men who were angry and unhappy and who genuinely believed in violence as a means to change the system. From our house on

B. K. Paul Avenue, I once saw soldiers cordoning off sensitive areas. We heard automatic weapons firing, what sounded like pistol shots and even bombs. Then we heard screams. This went on through the night. I myself was once stranded for hours, unable to enter my house as the area was cordoned off by paramilitary forces. They were Hindi-speaking, mostly from Punjab and Haryana and occasionally, learning that I came from the north, they would freely talk to me. Unable to comprehend any idealism in being a Naxal, the soldiers considered them anti-national, though even they regretted the loss of so many young lives.

The essence of Naxalbari, the movement that began in 1967 with farmers fighting landlords in a tiny patch of rural Bengal abutting the tea gardens, still lives as a reality check. So much so that while present-day armed revolutionaries call themselves Maoist, in public discourse they continue to be interchangeably known as Naxals or Naxalites. It is increasingly being accepted in top security and policy-making circles that India carries the potential to explode in a socio-economic cataclysm. Battles fought on account of inequality in standards of living and opportunity will continue to have increasingly greater purchase.

Questions are being raised about the government writing off millions of rupees in non-performing assets of banks but not the Rs 75 billion of farm indebtedness that could enhance the financial status of some 700 million Indians who depend on agriculture. Farmers are dying by the hundreds while the country follows the World Bank prescription of reducing subsidy to agriculture, to food, and handing over land to companies for cash crops.

Nobel Prize-winning economist Amartya Sen writes in *The Argumentative Indian*, 'The removal of poverty, particularly extreme poverty, calls for more participatory growth on a wide basis, which is not easy to achieve across the barriers of illiteracy, ill health, uncompleted land reforms and other sources of severe societal inequality.' If these issues are not addressed, the ideology that guided the Naxals may well spread.

Back to the 1972 Assembly elections: they found a place in the state's political memory for the wrong reasons. People saw the Congress stamping upon the democratic process of elections, engineering widespread rigging and indulging in open intimidation and coercion. The results were known even before votes were cast. The Congress won 216 seats; the CPI, teaming up with the Congress, won 35 seats and the Congress-led Progressive Democratic Alliance 254 seats out of a total of 280. The CPI(M) crashed to 14 and six other Left partners to a paltry 5 seats. However, the reduction in the share of votes for the CPI(M) was modest; a slide from 32 per cent to 28 per cent. It showed the deep roots the party had established in rural Bengal with its popular movements among peasants and labour.

Jyoti Basu has described the machinations of the Congress in his autobiography *Jotodur Mone Pore* thus: 'On 11 March, the day of polls, on reaching my Baranagar Constituency, I found that in most places voting was over. Of the 135 polling booths, the Congress had thrown out our polling agents in almost 100 booths. They snatched away the ballot boxes, stamped ballot papers in favour of the candidates of the right wing Communist Party (CPI) and stuffed them into the boxes.' This was Jyoti Basu's first and last defeat in a political career of over fifty years. I was at the Press Club when we heard the news that Jyoti Basu had withdrawn from the election, alleging rigging and corrupt practices by the Congress.

In protest, the elected Left MLAs boycotted the Assembly, calling the ministry headed by Siddhartha Sankar Ray an illegal one. During the five-year rule of the Congress from 1972 to 1977, which included two years of Emergency, the Left, particularly CPI(M) workers faced terrors as the state was awash with political violence. A culture of political killings, torture and 'disappearances' of opponents was the order of the day. The years between 1972 and 1977 were a very testing time for the CPI(M) as the party was being hounded and many of its leaders had to virtually go underground. Party workers fled their homes and deserted their neighbourhoods.

Indeed, the whole world seemed to be on the boil. Inspired by Vietnam's struggle, Calcutta resounded with '*Tomar naam, aamar naam, Vietnam Vietnam*' (Vietnam is your name, Vietnam is my name). There was no shortage of revolutionary inspiration. This was when a large number of ideologically committed and principled workers joined the CPI(M) with no hopes of position, patronage and perks. Most of the young CPI(M) leaders were the products of this period. With the opposition boycotting the Assembly, it was a smooth run for Siddhartha Sankar Ray's Congress government. It was expected that the uninterrupted five-year rule would give a fillip to the Congress, which would emerge strengthened. The story took a different turn with a massive Left Front victory in 1977.

The Emergency was lifted by Indira Gandhi and elections announced in 1977. A large section of West Bengal's CPI(M) was against participating in the polls. Memories of the farcical 1972 elections were still too fresh in their minds and there was little faith in the authenticity of the electoral process. The central committee of the CPI(M), however, decided to participate. The elections proved extremely significant: Indira Gandhi was defeated, putting to an end the thirty-year old rule of the Congress at the centre and giving birth to a coalition of diverse political parties, ranging from the right to the left.

There was a new power structure at the centre, with the Janata government headed by Morarji Desai and supported by the CPI(M) from the outside. A CPI(M)-led Left Front government took charge of West Bengal; the hammer-and-sickle-emblazoned flag of the Communist Party of India (Marxist) flying high in Calcutta. It was a great moment of relief, joy and euphoria for the Marxists.

The Left Front, consisting of the CPI(M), the Forward Bloc, the Revolutionary Socialist Party, the Marxist Forward Bloc and the Biplabi Bangla Congress, to its own utter surprise, won 231 seats and secured 54 per cent of the vote share in a 294-member Assembly. Interestingly, the CPI, as an ally of the Congress, was not a part of the Left Front in 1977. Even when their victory was stupendous, the Leftists were sceptical about being allowed to remain in power. The mighty Congress slid down to 20 seats, with a mere 23 per cent vote share. The poor showing of the Congress was largely due to Siddhartha Sankar Ray's style of governance and his sins of commission during the Emergency. More than 18,000 people had been rounded up under the Maintenance of Internal Security Act (MISA) in the state. They included senior journalists. I managed to escape by the skin of my teeth, but more on that later.

Asked why the Congress did so badly in West Bengal in 1977 despite being in power in the state from 1972 and given Siddhartha Sankar Ray's claim that no excesses were committed during Emergency under his rule, Saugata Roy, former union minister of state for urban development and a senior Trinamool party member said, 'It was largely due to rampant nepotism within the Congress. Sanjay Gandhi, who was all-powerful, disliked S.S. Ray and wanted to remove him as Chief Minister. Although Siddhartha babu survived, it was at a great cost. The Congress lost its credibility as a party.' Saugata Roy should know; he was general secretary of the West Bengal Pradesh Congress Committee for many years.

Thus in June 1977 came the moment of relief and euphoria for the victorious Marxists. Jyoti Basu had inherited a messed up state from his Congress predecessor. Expectations were running high. The

Communists at the time had a clean and pro-poor image, unlike their predecessors.

Perhaps the most vital task accomplished by the Communist government was land redistribution. It has been argued that this land reform, along with Operation Barga, provided the foundations for the Left Front's victory in subsequent elections.

Land reforms in West Bengal can be divided into two phases. In the first phase, from 1967 to 1970, Harekrishna Konar recovered around a million acres (4,000 square kilometres) of land through existing legal means. This was surplus land in excess of land ceiling laws held by big landowners and kept 'benami' (under false names). In the second phase, from 1978 to 1982, Benoy Choudhury accomplished two major tasks. The first was carried out under Operation Barga when around 1.7 million sharecroppers were formally recorded and assured of permanency of land holding and a fair share of the crop. The second task was the distribution of the million acres of land recovered earlier amongst 2.4 million poor and landless farm labourers. Thus, about four million people benefited directly from the land reforms.

As Operation Barga got off the ground, its impact could be seen in the outcome of the 1978 panchayat elections. The Left Front won 69 per cent of seats and gained 54 per cent of votes. The dominance of the landlords, rich peasants and moneylenders, who had been the bedrock of Congress support, was broken. For the first time in West Bengal, a democratic devolution of powers took place. The new leaders of the panchayats were not moneylenders or rich peasants. They were marginal farmers, primary or secondary teachers, unemployed young men, or landless agricultural labourers.

The panchayat elections of 1993 and 1998 showed that the Marxists retained their support base in the rural areas. The reason for these successive victories is to be found in the changed class relations, with the erstwhile power structure controlled by the landed gentry dismantled. The panchayats included a large number of the rural poor, marginal peasants, teachers, women and Dalits.

Thrice, in 1967 and again in 1970 and 1971, the United Front governments had been dismissed by the Congress government at the centre. The CPI(M) was evidently apprehensive of its future after the 1977 elections. Things, however, had changed at the centre. There was a Janata party government, and Indira Gandhi had personally lost in the elections following the Emergency. Within West Bengal too, both the Janata party and the Congress had been mauled badly in the elections. The Janata party, which had come to power at the centre and was hoping to sweep the polls in West Bengal, won only 29 seats.

The Congress on its part had split at the centre for the second time with the two factions getting their own symbols. The Indira-led Congress, now named Congress(I), got the symbol of the hand, while the splinter group came to be known as Congress(S). This further weakened the Congress in the state and its tally came down to 20 in the 1977 elections. The Congress was now a divided house with hardly any party machinery.

The Emergency had left an indelible imprint on the Indian psyche. Siddhartha Sankar Ray, who had accompanied Indira Gandhi to Rashtrapati Bhavan on the evening of 25 June 1975 to get the President's consent to declare a state of Emergency and who had publicly stated that Parliament's power of judicial review was 'preventing the emergence of a new economic order', was now openly against Indira Gandhi in the factional fight within the Congress. Ray contested the election to the post of Congress president and lost to Brahamanand Reddy.

Indeed, it was the excesses of the police, particularly during the Emergency in West Bengal with Siddhartha Ray at the helm—arrests of senior journalists, reckless demolitions and enforcement of press censorship—which largely contributed to the Congress debacle in the Assembly polls, from which it was never able to recover. It survived as a spineless organization. With an opposition completely decimated and showing little signs of recovery, the CPI(M) was able to look forward to a long tenure in office in West Bengal.

It would be fair to say, though, that while this massive Left victory was largely anti-incumbency in character, precipitated by Emergency excesses, it was also a positive vote in favour of the Left for the role that it had played in rehabilitating the refugees, in fighting for the peasantry and in improving the lot of school and college teachers. Undivided Bengal had witnessed a major struggle by the peasantry for the right to a one-third share of the crop in 1947-48. Known as the Tebhaga struggle, it was widely commented upon and became a subject of study in the national and the international press. The Communists played a critical role in this struggle, which gave them a firm foothold amongst the peasantry. It was, therefore, only to be expected that giving legal sanction to the right of the sharecroppers to one-third of the crop would be amongst the top priorities of the Left Front government when it took over. This well-planned and executed operation came to be known as Operation Barga.

Writing on the subject in the *Economic and Political Weekly* (13 October 2001), D. Bandopadhyay, the West Bengal revenue secretary who had been involved in the execution of the project under minister Benoy Chowdhury said, 'Operation Barga through which 1.2 million share croppers, who were in fact tenants were registered in the record of rights in just over three years (1978-81) thereby ensuring security of tenure, fairness of produce rent and heritable right of cultivation is considered both at home and abroad as a significant intervention of the Left Front government.'

The complete package comprised distribution of nearly one million acres of good agricultural land during the two United Front governments of 1967 and 1969-70 and free housing sites for the half million homeless families. It was a significant achievement and is reflected in the continuing upsurge in the state's agricultural output since 1983-84, breaking a century-old stagnation. This helped to consolidate the appeal of the Left Front to the peasantry who constitute the overwhelming majority of the electorate.

It was on this foundation that the Left Front government built the fortress that enabled it to survive for thirty-four years. In addition, there were steps taken to regularize the numerous refugee colonies that had sprung up on land grabbed earlier in the 1940s and 1950s. The CPI(M) thus secured an absolute majority on its own with 178 seats in the 1977 elections, which gradually led to a change for the government.

The Decline of the Congress

> Mrs Gandhi's autocratic control over the party and the impact it had in the states; the collapse of state party machinery, the hacking down of the party leaders and foisting her own candidates as party functionaries and chief ministers, the constant intervention in state politics and the disasters it caused, including operation Blue Star in Punjab, and the space she inadvertently created by her 'sense of personal insecurity' for other parties to rise.
>
> —Excerpts from *A Centenary History of Indian National Congress Volume V: 1964-1984,* by Prof Aditya Mukherjee, Director, Jawaharlal Nehru Institute of Advance Study

Matters could not have been in a greater state of disarray. While West Bengal was in the throes of political instability, the Congress at the centre was also in a state of confusion after the death of Jawaharlal Nehru on 27 May 1964. The home minister, Gulzarilal Nanda, was sworn in as the acting prime minister, an interim arrangement, and a permanent prime minister had to be elected. Kamaraj, then Congress president, consulted the party bosses in the states, popularly known as the Syndicate. The majority favoured Lal Bahadur Shastri. Morarji Desai, far more senior in years and regarded as a good administrator, was keen on contesting but was persuaded to withdraw.

It was during Shastri's tenure that another war with Pakistan started. Pakistan President Ayub Khan tried to repeat the same tactics that had been tried in 1947. Irregulars trained by the Pakistan army first entered Kashmir, hoping to start an uprising of the Kashmiris, who proved to be apathetic. Then a full-scale attack was launched by Pakistan, which led to some of the severest tank battles seen since World War II. The UN Security Council intervened and both sides agreed to a ceasefire. The Soviets organized the signing of the peace treaty at Tashkent. Tragically, Prime Minister Shastri died in his sleep of a heart attack the same night that he signed the peace treaty. Shastri's family, however, suspected that he had been poisoned. In fact, five years later, on 2 October1970 (Shastri's birthday), Lalita Shastri asked for a probe into her husband's death.

Lal Bahadur Shastri had his detractors who considered him too weak to manage a country as diverse as India. The war with Pakistan enhanced his stature and even critics within the party and outside commended him for his leadership. His death, however, threw open the question of who would be prime minister. Gulzarilal Nanda was sworn in as interim prime minister again. This time, however, Morarji Desai was determined to contest because the Syndicate and the Congress president were backing Indira Gandhi. In the ensuing contest, Indira Gandhi won easily.

The Nehru-Gandhi family was back in the saddle for the first time after the death of Nehru and with it began the long innings of Indira Gandhi. She had been chosen by the Syndicate, which believed that she would be pliable. How wrong they were! Within three weeks of Indira Gandhi's election as prime minister on 24 January 1966, an All-India Congress Committee (AICC) meeting was scheduled to take place in Jaipur. Some associates and I accompanied Ajoy Mukherjee and members of his group to that city. Our purpose was to apprise Indira Gandhi of the affairs in the West Bengal Congress where Atulya Ghosh, the strong man of the Congress and the president of the Pradesh Congress Committee, was at loggerheads with Ajoy Mukherjee.

The AICC meeting was an explosive one, with debates over the food distribution system, with the chief ministers of drought-affected states demanding an end to food zones and chief ministers of food surplus states shouting them down. The new prime minister tried to calm things down by making a statement on the subject but had to retreat. It was Congress president Kamaraj who intervened to have order restored.

Matters were too disturbed for Ajoy Mukherjee to receive any helpful hearing. Indira Gandhi herself was uncomfortable; she was wary of Nanda and had drifted apart from Kamaraj. The Syndicate that had made her prime minister was convinced that once the Lok Sabha elections, due in early 1967, were over, she would have to be removed. They wanted to hold their fire till then because she would be an asset for capturing votes. Speaking to a friend, Kamaraj commented on his mistake in making her the prime minister. 'A great man's daughter; a little man's great mistake,' he is reported to have said.

The country too was shadowed by severe drought, famine and acute food crisis. Rice riots were reported from West Bengal and Kerala. In the north-east, the Mizo tribes were in revolt; in Punjab, the demand for a separate state for Punjabi-speaking people had gained momentum. Sadhus and sanyasis had come out on the streets of Delhi demanding an end to cow slaughter. The economy was in a mess.

On 6 June 1966 Indira Gandhi announced the devaluation of the rupee. The monsoon failed once again and India faced a second year of drought. There was a major food crisis. In a symbolic gesture, Indira Gandhi gave up eating wheat and rice. West Bengal was facing its worst food crisis since 1959, when a peaceful rally of peasants had been subjected to a lathicharge that killed a large number of them. The opposition, mainly the Left parties, organized rallies and processions to protest against the food shortage. Chief Minister Prafulla Chandra Sen became the butt of jokes for having said that if people did not have rice they should eat bananas.

Meanwhile, my journalistic career had begun to take off. Initially, I was assistant editor of *Vichar Pravaha*, a Hindi fortnightly published by a group of four friends. It did not survive for more than a year, which was hardly surprising. We were all very young and inexperienced and full of idealism. Our articles aimed to show the path for the establishment of a socialistic society in the country. The articles were principled and ideological. Naturally, we had very few readers and still less by way of resources and advertising support. The end was expected but that did not kill our dreams.

Soon thereafter we started *Jan Sansar*, a Hindi weekly. I was assistant editor; wiser for the previous experience. The approach this time was more professional and pragmatic, though in keeping with our basic commitment to progressive and socialist policies. Later, I became editor of *Caldust*, a bi-colour tabloid-sized English weekly, which was well received both by readers and advertisers. At the same time, I was a special correspondent for the *Onlooker*, a popular English fortnightly, published from Bombay by the *Free Press Journal* group of newspapers.

The first decade (1962-1972) of my journalistic life was perhaps the most eventful period of post-Independence India. Three major wars took place during this period: with China in 1962, with Pakistan in 1965 and again in 1971, when Bangladesh was created. Nehru died in 1964, Shastri in 1966. The only contest ever held in the Congress Parliamentary Party to elect the prime minister took place on 19 January 1966 with Indira Gandhi winning by 355 votes to Morarji Desai's 169.

The 1967 elections saw a dramatic drop in the strength of the

Congress in the Lok Sabha. Worse, in the ensuing state elections, eight states were lost to the Congress for the first time. Indira Gandhi won but the Congress faced a debacle with all its strongmen in the states defeated: S.K. Patil in Maharashtra, Atulya Ghosh in West Bengal and Kamaraj in Tamil Nadu. The erosion of the Congress organization had begun, leading to the famous confrontation between Prime Minister Indira Gandhi and the Congress bosses led by its president Nijalingappa at the AICC meeting in Bangalore between July 10 and 13 in 1969 over the choice of the next President of India.

President Zakir Hussain had died in April 1969 and Indira Gandhi had put up Jagjivan Ram as her presidential candidate while the Syndicate chose Neelam Sanjeeva Reddy. Jagjivan Ram lost by one vote in the Congress Parliamentary Board. When the actual election took place Indira Gandhi called for a 'conscience vote', which resulted in the victory of V.V. Giri, who had stood as the non-official candidate supported by Indira Gandhi against the official Congress candidate, Sanjeeva Reddy. V.V. Giri won, but the Congress split.

Indira's Congress was known as Congress(R) while Nijalingappa's was known as Congress(O). The message was that the Syndicate, which had wanted a pliant prime minister, had been shown the door as Indira Gandhi quickly asserted her independence, emerging as a strong leader who took her own decisions. It was also an indication of what later characterized her style of functioning. Indira Gandhi chose to quickly assert her authority and win popular support through a number of steps. The first was nationalizing banks and then abolishing the privy purse (annual grants to India's royalty to compensate for the loss of their kingdoms in 1947).

Even as Indira was trying to get a hold on domestic matters, across the borders in Pakistan, a major crisis was brewing. In December 1970, Pakistan held its first general election based on adult franchise. In West Pakistan, Zulfiqar Ali Bhutto's Pakistan People's Party dominated. In the east, it was the National Awami League, led by Sheikh Mujibur Rahman. Yahya Khan, who had succeeded Ayub Khan as President and martial law administrator, had expected that Bhutto would win the elections and that he would continue as President. The results were a shock to both Yahya Khan and Bhutto. In West Pakistan, the PPP won 68 out of 144 seats while in East Pakistan, which had a much larger population, the National Awami League won 167 out of 169 seats.

East Pakistan had always been treated as a colony by the western part of the country. For both Bhutto and Yahya, the prospect of a Bengali, Mujibur Rahman, dominating Pakistan was unthinkable. Attempts to work out a settlement acceptable to West Pakistan were made but Mujib was not willing to submit. The repression that was then unleashed on the people of East Pakistan is well known. Following genocide, no less than 10 million refugees crossed the border to seek shelter in India. The majority was Hindu but there were quite a few Muslims, because all Bengali Muslims, especially the intellectuals, students and those in the Bengali media were special targets of attack. They sought shelter in West Bengal, Tripura and Meghalaya. The number of those killed ran into thousands.

The cost of providing shelter and food to these refugees was a burden that the Indian economy could ill afford to bear. Resistance to the Pakistan army and its local auxiliaries, the Razzakars, started with units of the East Pakistani army deserting and forming the core of a Mukti Bahini (liberation army). Disturbed by these developments, US President Richard Nixon dispatched his secretary of state, Henry Kissinger, to Beijing to formally establish relations with China. The US-Pakistan-China triangular axis was emerging as a threat to India.

To make the threat even more explicit, the US government dispatched a nuclear aircraft carrier to the Bay of Bengal. India's response was quick. On 17 August 1971, the Indo-Soviet Treaty of Peace, Friendship and Cooperation was signed. On 3 December, Pakistan made a pre-emptive strike on India's air bases in an unsuccessful attempt to cripple India's defence capability. The Indian army, having tasted the bitter fruit of defeat at the hands of the Chinese and learnt its lesson, was able to trap the bulk of the Pakistani forces in Bangladesh and force them to surrender. On 16 December, the Pakistani forces surrendered in Dhaka to Lt General Jagjit Singh Arora, Commander-in-Chief of the Eastern Command.

Bangladesh, a new state, was born. Indira Gandhi's handling of the situation and her courage in taking on Pakistan, despite threats from the US and China, were hailed by her own party and the opposition alike. Within her own party there was effusive praise for the prime minister and even Atal Bihari Vajpayee, the seniormost leader of the opposition party, the Bharatiya Janata Party and a Rajya Sabha member, spoke of her as 'Durga', the all-conquering goddess of Hindu mythology.

I recall a story of Indira Gandhi and the war, of which I was a silent observer. I was a member of a delegation of the Small Newspapers Association, which had an appointment with the prime minister in the evening of 3 December 1971 at Raj Bhavan in Calcutta. West Bengal governor Shanti Swarup Dhawan, a former judge of the Allahabad High Court, was briefing us on what points needed to be mentioned when we met the prime minister. Governor Dhawan was a progressive person and sympathetic to our cause and would have continued talking had not Indira Gandhi's press adviser, H.Y. Sharda Prasad, called us in. During our meeting with the prime minister, a slip was passed to her. She read it, did not react, and continued in her affable style. We later learnt that the note contained the news that Pakistan had started a war by attacking five of India's main air bases!

Before we went in to meet her, we were warned that the prime minister had only a few minutes for us. As soon as the introductions were over she asked, 'If you do not mind, can I sit in a relaxed manner?' She was in a very relaxed and friendly mood and seemed in no hurry. Sharda Prasad was also present. I remember asking her, 'How do you propose to implement your progressive and socialist programmes with a bureaucracy so deeply entrenched against such policies?' She gave a very straightforward and direct answer, 'All will have to change and will change. For this I need your support.' She was obviously disappointed with big newspapers and wanted to encourage the small ones.

Subinoy Das, a press photographer friend who was with us, wanted to be photographed with her. She agreed, saying, 'Normally I have a photograph with pressmen once a year on my birthday but let it be.' She then enquired who would take the photograph and I offered to do the honours. Subinoy, a very old friend, preserves the photograph with great pride. All this was taking place while she was actually internalizing the news that India was under military attack from Pakistan. I have often wondered with amazement about the ability of the lady to deal with such a grave situation with such equanimity, as she posed for a group photograph with us.

Indira Gandhi flew back that night. The Pakistan air force was airborne and there was a danger that the prime minister's plane, if identified, could be shot down. It is reported that on landing she told her secretary P.N. Dhar that she had not been sure of reaching Delhi. The report of our meeting was published in Pupul Jaykar's 1992 biography of Indira Gandhi: 'Indira was in Calcutta at the time. She had addressed a public meeting in the evening and was later on present at a gathering of writers, artists and literary personalities. Frantic efforts were made to contact her. It took two hours to locate the prime minister and give her the message. Her demeanour did not alter and she did not immediately react or end the meeting.'

I was involved, albeit in a small way, with the post-war rehabilitation effort. Along with some friends, I had gone to the Indo-East Pakistan border at Benapole on two occasions by local train from the Sealdah station, to hand over support materials to the Eastern Pakistan Rifles soldiers or the Mukti Bahini, as it was known. I met senior journalist Barun Sengupta at Benapol, whose dispatches from the border in the *Ananda Bazar Patrika* were very popular. I remember publishing a photograph of a receipt by the Eastern Pakistan Rifles acknowledging our material, in *Jan Sansar*.

I was also a member of the first press party to visit the border after the liberation of Bangladesh. Escorted by the Eastern Command, we left Calcutta early on 19 December three days after the surrender of the Pakistani forces. Our first stop was the Jessore cantonment where 90, 000 Pakistani prisoners of war were detained. I remember they were eating bananas and listening to transistors. We also went to the Khulna port, which had been devastated by the Indian navy. On the way we saw many dead bodies of Pakistani soldiers. Passing by were vehicles carrying Indian soldiers being wildly cheered by the Bangladeshis. I also saw local people carrying the heads of Pakistanis on rickshaws. We got ourselves photographed atop a T-72 Indian tank that was the mainstay of India's artillery in the Indo-Pak war of 1971.

It was an unforgettable journey and brings back many memories. Jiban Banerjee of the Bengali daily *Satyajug* was with us as we walked the streets of Jessore, which were full of enthusiastic, cheering crowds shouting, '*Sikh Sena Zindabad*' (Long live the Sikh soldiers; the Sikh regiment of the Indian army had been deployed there); '*Joy Bangla*' and '*Joy Mukti Bahini*'. On the day of victory, 16 December, Calcutta went berserk with jubilation. Shouts of '*Joy Bangla*' filled the air, throughout the night. Huge processions came out on the street, disregarding the black-out. The sight of unknown people congratulating and embracing each other is etched in my memory.

It is often said that victory does not spare the victor. Hardly a year had passed since the war victory and the triumph of the Congress in the 1971 polls—including in West Bengal—before widespread social and economic discontent rapidly engulfed the country. Before examining the consequences of that discontent, it is necessary to understand the extent of the victory scored by Indira Gandhi in the elections. Without this massive victory she could not have had the confidence to take the bold decision that she did over aiding the dismemberment of Pakistan and the formation of Bangladesh.

Indira Gandhi's frustration after becoming prime minister was palpable. Within the party there was pressure from Morarji Desai, who wanted to be prime minister; the Syndicate too was making it difficult for her to function and to emerge as the prime minister in her own right. Even the opposition felt that the young and inexperienced Indira would only be a puppet in the hands of the power brokers in the Congress. Ram Manohar Lohia called her a '*gungi gudiya*' (a dumb doll). Her success in defeating the official nominee for the presidential election in August 1969 and getting V.V. Giri elected changed all that. Indira Gandhi had gained in confidence.

To remove the impediments that stood in the way of her functioning as prime minister once and for all, she decided to call early elections to the Lok Sabha, 14 months ahead of schedule. Countering the election cry of her opponents: 'Indira *hatao*' (remove Indira), she came up with the brilliant slogan, '*Garibi hatao*' (remove poverty). Indira's Congress (the Congress(R), formed after her expulsion from the Congress for having defied the Syndicate and not backing the official presidential candidate), won a resounding victory with 352 seats of a total of 518 in the Lok Sabha. The Congress(O), as the official Congress called itself after the split, was practically wiped out.

The real reasons for the people's discontent with the Congress, however, survived despite Indira Gandhi's attempt to give a socialist orientation to Congress policies by nationalizing the banks and abolishing the privy purses. The sufferings of the masses worsened. Repeated failure of the monsoons, inflation, rising international oil prices, labour unrest, strikes in urban areas, fall in production, closure of factories, increasing corruption, empty grain bins and the all-time low balance in the treasury had hit all sections of the people—not only the poor but the middle class as well.

There were other serious problems too. Jaiprakash Narayan's Youth for Democracy students' movement that later turned into the '*Sampoorn Kranti Andolan*' (total revolution movement) took root against corruption in Bihar and Gujarat. Morarji Desai started a fast unto death demanding fresh polls in Gujarat, a railway strike disrupted the movement of essential commodities, the arrest of a large number of railway workers and the eviction of their families from their quarters all added to the popular discontent. Jaiprakash's movement evoked a wide response and his meetings drew huge crowds.

Then came a devastating blow for Indira Gandhi. Her election—challenged in the Allahabad High Court by her defeated opponent Raj Narain on grounds of corrupt practices—was countermanded. She was disqualified from contesting elections for six years. Indira Gandhi might have thought of resigning but her son Sanjay and

Siddhartha Sankar Ray advised her to continue as prime minister. As a lawyer, Siddhartha Ray suggested that there were provisions in the Constitution under which a state of Emergency could be imposed. This was what she finally agreed to.

On 25 June 1975 the ordinance declaring the Emergency was drafted with the help of Siddhartha Sankar Ray and signed by the pliant president Fakhruddin Ali Ahmed. The same night, opposition leaders were put into jail. Newspapers were prevented from bringing out the morning's paper by switching off their power supply. The next morning, All India Radio announced the declaration of a state of Emergency and the suspension of all civil liberties in India.

The Emergency marked another turning point in the post-Independence history of India. It not only proved disastrous for the Congress but for the country as a whole. While there has been some revival in the fortunes of the party after the disastrous results in the 1977 elections, when even Indira Gandhi was defeated, it lost its stature and has never quite regained it. In many states, it has been reduced to a minuscule minority.

The Janata government came to power at the centre in 1977, but it did not last long. In the 1980 elections, the Congress led by Indira Gandhi returned to power. It won 353 seats, one more than it did with the *garibi hatao* campaign of 1971. However, the country was facing numerous problems and one of them threatened to tear apart the north of the country. In Punjab, Jarnail Singh Bhindranwale, a Sikh extremist, had gradually gained strength and had been able to enter the Akal Takht, the highest seat of temporal authority in Sikhism, at the Golden Temple, which he had turned into a fortress. He had declared that the Sikhs were a separate 'qaum', which could be interpreted as claiming separate nationhood for the Sikhs.

With the situation getting out of hand, Prime Minister Indira Gandhi decided to take action. Operation Blue Star was launched to flush out the extremists holding out in the Golden Temple in Amritsar. The army succeeded in doing so and in the operation both Bhindranwale and his lieutenant Shubeg Singh, a former major general of the Indian army, were killed.

There was an agonizing backlash amongst the Sikhs, which was controlled after some time. With the Harmander Saheb, the holiest of the Sikh Shrines being severely mauled the sentiments of the Sikh community were deeply hurt. The operation caused a deep wound in the Sikh psyche. The three weeks following operation Bluestar did not in any way lead to a return to normalcy. The army continued to occupy the Golden Temple precincts and villages all over Punjab. The Akalis gave a call for 'Shahidi Jathas' (Martyrs' groups) for a massive protest on 15 July 1984. Punjab crisis became more serious on 1 September 1984 when 300 unarmed youth misbehaved in the gurudwara at Darshni Dori and some alleged terrorists had physically thrown out the granthis (those who recite the Sikh holy scriptures). The most lethal consequence of Operation Blue Star was that two of Indira Gandhi's Sikh security guards shot her at point blank range. She died on her way to the hospital on 31 October 1984.

This was followed by one of the most shameful episodes in the post-independence history of the country. Mobs crying for revenge surrounded the homes of Sikhs and more than a thousand were killed in Delhi alone. In Uttar Pradesh and in many other cities across the country, similar attacks took place on the Sikhs. However, as Ramchandra Guha reports: 'One city where the violence was minimal was Calcutta. There were 50,000 Sikhs in the city...very few were harmed and not one died. Jyoti Basu had ordered the police to ensure that peace be maintained. The instructions were honoured with the city's powerful trade unions keeping an eye.'

The power of the land reforms continued to serve the Left well as they continued to fight for peasant rights and carry out important land reforms. The goodwill engendered by their performance on the communal harmony front also helped at the polls. Thus, when at the centre the Congress won as many as 404 seats in the Lok Sabha election in 1984, exceeding all past records including that of Rajiv Gandhi's maternal grandfather, Jawaharlal Nehru, in the election to the West Bengal state Assembly, held three years later in 1987, the Left Front increased its tally, from 238 seats in 1982, to 251.

The damage done during Indira Gandhi's reign to the country's institutions has been such that it is difficult to fathom when and how it will ever be repaired. Corruption at all levels has reached enormous proportions. The state of affairs of the party during Indira Gandhi's time is best explained in an essay in the recently published *A Centenary History of Indian National Congress Volume V 1964-1984*, brought out by the party itself.

The book has created such controversy that the head of its editorial board, then senior Congress minister and currently President of India, Pranab Mukherjee, was forced to explain that, 'it is not an official history.' Nor is it 'a party's perspective'. Its aim, he said, is to 'generate an objective and scholarly perspective for the period.' However, Sonia Gandhi, in her foreword to the volume said, 'it provides a chance to clear the air and set the record straight. Many decisions taken during that period were enveloped in partisan political debate.'

Some observations of historians and eminent journalists in the volume are worth quoting. 'Mrs Gandhi's autocratic control over the party and the impact it had in the states; the collapse of state party machinery; the hacking down of the party leaders and foisting her own candidates as party functionaries and chief ministers; the constant intervention in state politics and the disasters it caused, including Operation Blue Star in Punjab, and the space she inadvertently created by her 'sense of personal insecurity' for other parties to rise,' wrote Sudha Pai, political studies professor at JNU.

Veteran journalist Inder Malhotra was even more acerbic: 'After her rise to supremacy...a courtier culture grew fast and spawned rampant sycophancy... It was a surprise that someone of her sophistication...could tolerate the crudest flattery as each of the competing courtiers tried to outdo each other to catch the benign attention of the sole dispenser of patronage; backbiting, backstabbing and intrigue became the order of the day.'

Historian Bipan Chandra, the editor of the volume, wrote, 'Having emasculated the Congress...and having no other organization to rely upon, Mrs Gandhi and the central and state governments depended almost entirely on the bureaucracy and the police... for routine administration of the 20-point and family planning programme. What is surprising...is why someone as sensitive, imaginative and politically shrewd as Mrs Gandhi failed to perceive the gravity of the situation and did not provide a healing touch, especially when the poor, her major political power base, were being alienated...by the Sanjay factor.'

In West Bengal, after intermittent periods of President's Rule, elections were held in 1972 in an atmosphere of turmoil and splits in different parties while the common people continued to suffer from food shortages, power cuts, high prices, economic decline and a total lack of governance. Writing on the elections, Ramachandra Guha says in his book *India After Gandhi*, 'In at least one state the presence and example of the prime minister was not enough. This was West Bengal, where the Congress won only with resort to a mixture of terror, intimidation and fraud. Gangs of hooligans stuffed ballot boxes with the police idly looking on. There was 'mass-scale rigging' in Calcutta, as one activist recalled, *goondas* paid by the Congress told voters assembled outside polling stations that they might as well go home, since they had already cast all the registered votes. Now in alliance with the CPI, the Congress captured 251 out of 280 seats in the Assembly.'

During the Emergency, Siddhartha Sankar Ray had spoken against Sanjay to Indira Gandhi and said that his involvement in the Maruti project was doing harm to her image. Sanjay got to know about this, as Indira Gandhi would not keep anything from him. Sanjay took it as Ray's personal animosity towards him and wanted to get rid of Ray as chief minister of West Bengal. Sanjay had begun to dislike Ray and the dislike between the two was mutual. When Sanjay visited Calcutta during Siddhartha Ray's tenure as chief minister, he did not get the attention that he felt he deserved. Sanjay was, therefore, despite Indira Gandhi's disagreement, keen to remove Siddhartha as chief minister and many alternative names were being considered. Pranab Mukherjee, ABA Ghani Khan Chowdhury and even Gopal Das Nag were considered, amongst others. Siddhartha Sankar Ray's role in helping Mrs Gandhi to bring in the Emergency and in imposing it in West Bengal had been noted by the electorate in West Bengal, as were the after-effects of its imposition.

It was during the Emergency that *Caldust* carried the story 'West Bengal Scene: Hectic Political Activities' in its 12 September 1976 issue. The story talked about Chief Minister Ray losing the support of the Congress high command and the possibility of his being replaced by Pranab Mukherjee with the blessings of Sanjay Gandhi. As I was close to many senior central Congress leaders and an admirer of Indira Gandhi, my weekly was exempted from censorship under the instructions of Vidya Charan Shukla, then union information and broadcasting minister. I was thus free to publish political stories.

I realized, however, that for Siddhartha Babu there could be no exceptions. Copies of the weekly were picked up from the vendors. Pritin Bhattacharya, press secretary to Siddhartha Sankar Ray, made a threatening phone call summoning me to his office. The police was chasing me and I evaded arrest with the help of a veteran and highly respected central minister. In its issue of 2 November 2009, the news magazine *Outlook* published an interview with Siddhartha Sankar Ray about his role during the Emergency, in which he claimed that nobody was arrested in Calcutta during the Emergency!

Refuting this statement, I wrote a letter to the editor, which was published by *Outlook* in its issue of 16 November 2009 as follows:

> 'Mr S.S. Ray said that "I had declared that nobody would be arrested in Calcutta" in his interview to your magazine but I had a very frightening experience as the editor of the *Caldust* English Weekly published from Calcutta in 1976. The police visited my office to confiscate all the copies of the weekly dated 12 September 1976, which carried a political story captioned, "West Bengal Scene: Hectic Political Activities" about Ray losing the support of the Congress high command and the likelihood of him being replaced by Pranab Mukherjee as the West Bengal CM at the insistance of Sanjay Gandhi. Ray's Press secretary, Pritin Bhattacharya, made threatening phone calls reminding me about the Emergency and censorship. The police was after me. I was saved from being arrested due to the intervention of the then Union petroleum minister, K.D. Malviya. It is well-known that two senior journalists, namely Barun Sengupta and Gourkishore Ghosh, were put behind bars for two months during the Emergency.'

Analysing the fall of the Congress in the 1970s, Om Prakash Mishra, general secretary and spokesperson of the West Bengal Pradesh Congress Committee, said, 'In the wake of the Emergency, the Congress had lost its credibility and, with factionalism running very high, the party was divided and demoralized.' With the return of Indira Gandhi to power at the centre in 1980, the state Congress was revived and, despite the implementation of Panchayati Raj by the CPI(M), the Congress secured 42 per cent of votes in the 1982 Assembly elections, forcing the Left to realize that the Congress needed to be politically challenged. Instead, the CPI(M) indulged in electoral malpractices to win the elections, improving the Left Front's tally from 231 to 238 in the 1982 Assembly polls, thus retaining its three-fourths majority. The Congress(I) and the Congress(S) merged after the elections and, with a combined strength of 53 seats, got the status of opposition party in the Assembly. Even in the Lok Sabha polls in 1980 and 1984, however, the Congress fared satisfactorily. Then came the decline.

Call it strategic management of the opposition by the CPI(M) or what you will, the Congress withered in West Bengal. Its vote share went down in the 1987 Assembly elections. 'Somen Mitra and Subrata Mukherjee were youngish, reckless and only based in Calcutta. Priya Ranjan Das Munshi, with his earlier resignation from the Congress, had lost his hold and credibility, Siddhartha Sankar Ray was out and Barkat Ghani Khan Chowdhury was loud on rhetoric and weak on delivery. Somen was all-powerful. Even so, in the election of PCC president in 1982, Mamata Banerjee lost to Somen by only 28 votes. With intensified inner struggle, the Congress became weak, benefitting the Left Front,' explained Om Prakash Mishra.

'Many of us left the Congress and joined the TMC because Mamata Banerjee, with her consistent and persistent opposition and struggle against the Left Front, was more acceptable to the people as an anti-Left force than the Congress. The credibility of the Congress as an anti-Left force was low,' said Sudip Bandyopadhay, TMC Member of Parliament from North Kolkata. Sudip Bandyopadhay, as chief whip of the TMC in the Lok Sabha, has emerged as the voice of Mamata in Delhi.

A five-term MLA who, in his first election to the Lok Sabha in 2009, defeated CPI(M) stalwart Mohammad Salim, Sudip Bandyopadhay is confident that the TMC government will not only complete its term but will also be re-elected in 2016. 'I can see at least a 10-year term if not more for our government in the state. Mamata will also play an important role in national politics. The 2014 parliamentary polls will throw up surprises and the TMC will emerge as a major power.'

Tracing the history of the split of the state Congress and the formation of the TMC, Mishra said that the seeds were sown during the 1982 elections for the PCC president between Somen and Mamata, while the actual split took place in 1998. Mishra believes that Mamata harmed the Congress more than the CPI(M) in the 1998 Lok Sabha polls, with the Left Front maintaining its tally of 33 seats in 1996 while the Congress was reduced to a paltry single seat. The TMC bagged 7 seats. It was during these elections that the BJP won its first parliamentary seat since 1952 from Dum Dum, with the support of the TMC. In the 1999 Lok Sabha polls, the TMC improved its strength in the Lok Sabha from 7 to 8 but, after joining the BJP-led National Democratic Alliance, Mamata was in the wilderness for many years and, in the 2004 Lok Sabha polls, she only won a single seat: her own. The Congress doubled its tally of 3 in 1999 to 6 in the 2004 Parliamentary polls. It was strongly rumoured around this time that a big industrial house had contributed Rs 26 crore to Mamata's election fund to organize the split and break the Congress.

New Industrial Policy: Basu as Bengal's Deng

> I don't care if it's a white cat or a black cat.
> It's a good cat as long as it catches mice.
> —Deng Tsiaoping in 1961, at the Guangzhou conference of the Communist Party of China

While the Left Front was in its third term (1987-1992) as the ruling coalition in West Bengal, some major changes were taking place around the world. Although in far-off China and the Soviet Union, they had repercussions on the politics and economics of India, particularly in West Bengal. While the Brezhnev era witnessed a growth in the military might of the Soviet Union, it was also a period of economic stagnation for that country. In the Cold War, with the United States and the NATO powers ranged on one side and the Soviet Union with its East European allies on the other, the Soviet Union was being forced to allocate an extraordinarily large percentage of its budget and its productive capacity to its armed forces. This resulted in a shortage of consumer goods and in particular, a shortage of food. This was leading to growing dissatisfaction among its population.

Economic stagnation had hit the East European countries too and they were getting restive. Not popular at the best of times—as the Communist regimes in those countries had been foisted on them after the Molotov Ribbentrop pact signed in August 1939—the governments of those countries were becoming increasingly isolated from the masses. It was under Brezhnev too that direct military intervention in Afghanistan took place—in the face of resistance from the local people aided by the Mujahideen and supported by Pakistan and the United States—leading to a severe strain on the resources of the Soviet Union.

Realizing that drastic measures were needed to shore up the Soviet economy and to prevent the unrest within the country from getting out of control, Gorbachev, who took over as general secretary of the CPSU in 1985, decided to make a departure in both its economic and political policies with his *glasnost* (freedom and transparency) and *perestroika* (reconstruction and economic reforms). However, this had unintended consequences and resulted in a cascade of events that eventually concluded with the dissolution of the Soviet Union in 1991. In the East European countries too, beginning with Poland, Communist regimes were overthrown in one country after another.

The consequence of these events in the international sphere was the end of the Cold War, with the United States of America emerging as the sole global superpower. Perhaps an even more far-reaching consequence was that it was generally interpreted as a failure of socialism. In fact, it led to an American political scientist, Francis Fukuyama, coming out with the thesis that the end of history had been reached and capitalism was there to stay as long as mankind remained on the planet.

The Constitution of India had, in the original version in 1950, described India as a 'sovereign, democratic republic'. The words 'socialist' and 'secular' were added later in 1976 through the 42nd amendment to the Constitution. Personally, I had been a staunch supporter of socialism though not of the Communist variety. I had been close to socialist and progressive leaders in the Congress and had even been part of the Congress Socialist Forum.

Jolly Mohan Kaul, veteran journalist but, more importantly, once the Calcutta district secretary of the undivided Communist Party of India, used to write the last page of *Caldust*, called Karvan-e-hayat, under the pseudonym Al-Birauni. In his column in the issue of 26 September 1976, he described the 42nd Constitutional amendment as 'a powerful instrument to achieve socialism'. He wrote, 'The goal may still be a long way off. But the fact that we have been able to set our sights clearly is in itself a significant step forward... The unambiguous declaration that the New Bill proposes to make in the preamble to our Constitution does mark a watershed in the post-independence political history of India.'

By the 1980s though, the rigid controls and the corruption-ridden 'licence raj' had brought the economy to a state of bankruptcy. There was a growing realization that change was necessary. The collapse of the Soviet Union strengthened this feeling and opened the way for economic reforms. Manmohan Singh, inducted as finance minister in June 1991 by Prime Minister Narasimha Rao, launched a series of reforms that unshackled the economy in the 1990s.

There were far reaching and multi-layered consequences, but over the next two decades of the reforms, India, along with China, has emerged as a leading economic power, albeit amidst growing economic disparities at home. The two countries seem poised to become the new global superpowers of the 21st century, despite the many structural imbalances within their domestic systems. There is little doubt that Manmohan Singh's economic reforms would not have received the ready acceptance that they did had the collapse of the Soviet experiment in socialism not made nationalist opinion in the country receptive to the idea. I was among those who realized that the just and humane society that I had dreamed of in my younger days could not be achieved through the rigid controls and curbs on entrepreneurial freedom and initiative that had become a feature of our political system in the 1960s and 1970s.

It was at this crucial juncture that, as secretary general of Webfuna, I organized a two-day seminar on the role of foreign capital. The seminar was held on 28 July 1990 in Calcutta, even before Manmohan Singh initiated his economic reforms. The seminar was inaugurated by Biju Patnaik, the chief minister of Orissa; Russi Mody, chairman of Tata Steel, delivered the keynote address; the union minister of state for industry, Srikant Jena, was the chief guest; while Hashim Abdul Halim, Speaker of the West Bengal Assembly, presided. Halim's active support also reflected the changing views of the Left Front on foreign capital.

Initially, West Bengal Chief Minister Jyoti Basu had agreed to inaugurate the seminar but some pressing engagement made him drop out almost at the last moment. There was unfounded speculation that Jyoti Basu had backed out due to pressure from party hardliners. Biju Patnaik was highly disappointed over the absence of Jyoti Basu, and said so, 'His presence would have been important and I was looking forward to holding some important discussions with him.'

No doubt Basu's failures in his first two terms from 1977 to 1987 on industrial front were too many and too serious for any history to gloss over. However, it was only Jyoti Basu who first initiated policies to attract Indian and foreign investment to Bengal. He had decency, a sense of proportion and an amiable gentleman. This helped him to somehow bring private and Central government investment. He presided over the leftist success with land reforms and panchayats. It was his new approach towards private capital which was carried forward by his successor Buddhadev Bhattacharya.

Speakers at different sessions included Erling Desau, resident representative of the United Nations Development Programme (UNDP), New Delhi; Matiul Islam, a Bangladeshi national and country director, United Nations Industrial Development Organization (UNIDO), who delivered one of the best speeches at the seminar; Amitava Ghosh, deputy governor, Reserve Bank of India, J.V. Shetty, chairman, United Bank of India; Abhijit Sen, president, Bengal Chamber of Commerce and Industry and N. Sitaraman, director, ITC Ltd. The success of the seminar and the wide response it received, contributed to some extent, I venture to think, towards an understanding of the era of economic reforms in India.

As a follow up, Webfuna organized a national seminar on India's foreign trade in April 1993. It was inaugurated by Governor of West Bengal S. Narul Hasan. Pranab Mukherjee, then commerce minister, was the chief guest. Russi Mody was the keynote speaker and this time the government of West Bengal not only supported the initiative but also actively participated in the seminar. Commerce and industry minister Bidyut Ganguly, the chairman of the West Bengal Industrial Development Corporation Tarun Dutta, and A.C. Roy, chairman of the Calcutta Port Trust were speakers. Clearly, mind-sets were changing within the Left Front government.

However, the Left in West Bengal still seemed reluctant to give up the old line—the old policy of militant labour movement, anti-capital attitude and the policy of abolishing study of English from primary schools—though there were indications that Jyoti Basu had begun to think differently. Continuing my efforts to encourage industrial development in West Bengal, we decided that Webfuna would collaborate with the state commerce and industry department to hold a one-day workshop on 'Prospects and Problems of Industrial Development in West Bengal' in August

1994. The response from the government was surprisingly good. Several ministers, including industry and labour ministers, Bidyut Ganguly and Shanti Ghatak and government officials including the chief secretary and the power secretary confirmed their participation in different sessions. Yet there were bureaucrats who were keen to create obstacles, as I was to learn later.

I had invited Jyoti Basu to inaugurate the seminar. Nearer the date of the workshop, a gentle enquiry was made by the industry department as to who would deliver the keynote address on behalf of industry. I did not take this seriously and casually informed the department that various names were under consideration but we would like to have someone who could talk about the prospects as well as the problems that industrialists were facing in their efforts to expand in West Bengal.

Before we could finalize a name, the department proposed a panel of three industrialists from which we could choose the keynote speaker. All of them were known to be pro-government businessmen and lacked the stature and position to make an independent statement. I finally decided on Federation of Indian Chambers of Commerce and Industry (FICCI) president A.K. Rungta. When I approached him, he asked if his name had been cleared by the government. 'The programme is being organized jointly with the West Bengal government, that too at the Assembly House, and I am a known critic of their policies,' he said.

I told him that even though his name had not been cleared, I felt that as long as he was not biased there should not be any problem. As organizers we had every right to choose the speaker on behalf of the industrial sector. Even though I did not anticipate a problem, I made discreet enquiries and was given a hint that if A.K. Rungta was invited, Jyoti Basu might not attend. I found this difficult to believe and felt that this must be the machination of hardliners.

I discussed the matter at the appropriate level and was assured that I had the right to choose the speakers. The conference was a grand success and the FICCI president, as expected, made critical references to the industrial policy of West Bengal, to which Jyoti Basu responded suitably, not forgetting to refer to the shortcomings and failures.

The workshop created enough interest in business circles and in the media as well. The *Financial Express* said in its story, 'Basu, FICCI Chief clash over State prospects', quoting A.K. Rungta as saying, 'How do you expect them (foreign companies) to believe that doors would be open to them in this state where the state government happens to be a staunch opponent of the centre's opening-up policies?' The report, however, added, 'In a significant move Jyoti Basu praised the Rao government and specially Dr Manmohan Singh for some of their moves and policies. The Bakreshwar Thermal Power Project could not have taken a concrete shape without the cooperation of Dr Singh in particular and the centre as a whole. Basu also welcomed the initiation of de-licencing as without it he said there would be discrimination between states.'

The state commerce and industry minister, Bidyut Ganguly, said that the fund-starved state government, in its desperate bid to woo investors, was providing a number of incentives and special facilities to them. Referring to the FICCI chief's contention that industrialists were averse to coming to this part of the country primarily because of labour problems and low productivity of the work force, Bidyut Ganguly said that the state government was aware of some untoward incidences in some industrial complexes and was trying to work out a corrective measure for it. As organizers, we were happy that the workshop had served its purpose of hosting an open and frank discussion on both the prospects and problems of industrial development in the state.

Bureaucrats play a very important role in the success and failure of governments and hiding failures help neither the bureaucracy nor the rulers. Unfortunately, in our political system, rarely can support be distinguished from sycophancy, which is perhaps a reflection of the leaders. In fact, bureaucrats need to be encouraged to place the truth, however unpleasant, before the government. The Left Front, no different from other governments, encouraged sycophancy instead. Interestingly the FICCI president, in the course of his speech, talked about his visit to China. He emphasized that China was a Communist country, trying to industrialize rapidly and suggested that West Bengal too adopt the same industrial policy.

China's economic growth has been very rapid since Deng Tsiaoping took over. Economists estimate that China's gross domestic product (GDP) growth between 1978 and 2005 was at 9.5 per cent a year. China's GDP during this period rose 10-fold reaching $2.6 trillion in 2006, exceeded only by the USA, Japan and Germany. There was sharp increase in the Chinese GDP, rising from Rmb 362.4 billion in 1978 at the start of the reform period to Rmb 30 trillion in 2008. Although the global economic crisis has reduced China's growth rate, it is still healthy at between 9 and 10 per cent. China has emerged as a major economic power. The Chinese economy may equal or even surpass that of the USA in the next decades.

In the face of these developments, Jyoti Basu formulated a new industrial policy for West Bengal, which was no different from the liberalization policy adopted by the central government. Despite reluctance of his Left Front partners, he pushed this policy, ignoring the murmurs of some of his ministerial colleagues. With the example of China staring them in the face, Jyoti Basu pushed through his policy and won the sobriquet of 'the Deng of West Bengal'.

There was, of course, a flipside to this tilt towards industry. With growing closeness of the Left Front, particularly the CPI(M), to industry and industrialists and with Deng reportedly saying, 'to be rich is good', the inhibitions that had prompted earlier generations of Communists to maintain a frugal lifestyle and to abhor ostentation disappeared. The housing construction boom and the growth of the promoters' and developers' lobby opened up opportunities to get rich quickly. Corruption became endemic in sections of the Left parties.

Thus, as the decade of the 1980s ended and the central government itself embraced globalization and all that went with it, in West Bengal a Left government led by the Communists got entangled in the worldwide net of neo-liberal capitalism. The consequences of this will reveal themselves in the pages that follow.

The Beginning of the End

> A man can fall many times, but he is not a failure until he begins to blame somebody else.
>
> —John Burroughs

It may be a cliché that absolute power corrupts absolutely, but it can be held true for the Left in West Bengal. It was the decimation of the opposition in the state that strengthened those elements in the CPI(M) that believed in strong arm tactics to stifle all dissent. It also explains perhaps why—just when the government was taking measures such as Operation Barga to secure their base among the peasants and the regularization of refugee colonies to gather popular support—they started to use draconian measures to evict a group of refugees from the island of Marichjhapi in the Sunderbans area of West Bengal in 1978-79. This happened soon after the Left Front came to power in West Bengal.

Since the press had been prevented from reaching the remote area and covering the event, it was left to those refugees who had managed to escape and to reveal all that had happened. A few have ventured to collect these accounts and to put them in print. The Fact Finding Mission (FFM) organized by the People's Coalition on Food Sovereignty is one such example.

Although it is alleged that this whole operation was conceived, planned and executed by the CPI(M) leadership, one wonders whether the other partners in the Left Front were aware and, if so, whether they protested or even discussed the issue. The CPI(M)'s domination of the Left Front had already become so well established that the other partners were probably not informed, or perhaps given a doctored version of the events. There was no coverage in the media. It would appear that for the Bengali masses, the Left could do no wrong. Yet there was wrongdoing everywhere.

During its first two terms in office, the CPI(M) was still a little tentative about its future and was more concerned with implementing its development agenda, which it had championed during the years when it was in opposition. Simultaneously, however, it began implementing another agenda: to consolidate its hold on the government and to perpetuate a one-party rule in states where it was in power. For this the party set out to capture all institutions, beginning with the most important—the educational institutions. Technically, it was a coalition of different Left parties but the CPI(M)'s domination was so overwhelming that other partners hardly dared to express dissent.

As many of the other partners of the Front have subsequently stated, many important decisions of the Left Front government—not just Marichjhapi—were taken without consulting or even informing the other partners. Capturing trade unions was another part of the agenda. Not only did they seek control of trade unions under the influence of the Indian National Trade Union Congress (INTUC), even unions run by its Front partners such as the CPI, the Forward Bloc and the RSP were attacked and taken over. The most damaging part of the CPI(M)'s programme was the way in which educational institutions were sought to be made fiefdoms of the ruling party.

The classic case is that of Calcutta University, a hallowed institution, which even under British rule had national stalwarts as vice-chancellors: Gooroodas Bannerjee, Nilratan Sarkar, Bhupendranath Bose, Jadunath Sarkar and Ashutosh Mukherji. Under their leadership it became the breeding ground of outstanding scholars such as Jagadis Chandra Bose, Meghnad Saha, Abanindranath Tagore, Debdatta Bhandarkar, Sarvapalli Radhakrishnan and Ramesh Chandra Mazumdar. In a remarkable book titled *Red Hammer Over Calcutta University*, former vice-chancellor Santosh Bhattacharya chronicles the story of how this great institution was laid siege to just because a vice-chancellor of the party's choice was not appointed.

The book is replete with documents, copies of correspondence between the vice-chancellor and the government. Bhattacharya begins by pointing out how they made desperate attempts to prevent him for standing for the election. 'After my candidature became public, the CPI(M) went into top gear for marshalling votes but found the ground shaky.' The party then tried to persuade him to withdraw using the bait of offering other equally honourable positions if he agreed to their suggestion. An emissary from the top leadership of the party came to him with a suggestion.

'Of course, I considered this as a bribe and seethed with anger because they ought to have known from my past that my beliefs were not for trade,' writes Bhattacharya. The election held on 7 December 1982 created history, and had repercussions far and wide. In the panel of three names presented to the senate for the selection of the next vice-chancellor, Bhattacharya not only got through but secured the highest votes, 40 as against 35 secured by Left Front candidate Ramen Poddar. Efforts were then made to get the chancellor, Governor B.D. Pande, to appoint Poddar based on the recommendation of the higher education minister.

West Bengal's literati waited with bated breath for the chancellor's decision. On 30 December 1983, the chancellor's letter appointing

Santosh Bhattacharya was communicated to the secretary for higher education who sent the letter of appointment the same day. From that day began a battle with the CPI(M), who vowed that it would not let him function. 'About a week before I joined as the vice-chancellor, emissaries of the CPI(M), personally known to me for a long time, had threatened that they would not allow me to function.'

They kept their word. Over the three years of his term, from 1984–1987, they used every method to prevent him from functioning. Cadres belonging to the employees' union would gherao him, use abusive language and stop his car from entering or leaving. The same treatment was meted out to some of the officers who tried to implement his directives. These incidents were regularly reported in the daily press. Newspapers like *The Statesman* and *Ananda Bazar Patrika* wrote editorials decrying the blatant use of muscle power and other methods to prevent a legally appointed vice-chancellor, a person held in high regard in academic circles, from functioning. Even his attempts to appoint a pro-vice chancellor—the prerogative of the vice-chancellor—were blocked.

'The registrar became famous overnight for his audacity in writing "take back your order" on my written order for appointing two special officers even though it was a standard practice in the University and the vice-chancellor was empowered for the purpose,' writes Santosh Bhattacharya. His first salary was held up. A committee was set up to find out what went wrong. It reported that the registrar had not carried out his responsibility in the matter. 'Perhaps the CPM's parallel organization thought that I would not be able to stick out even for a month and the salary bill would not be required.' Ultimately the VC had to start functioning from his home and even this was challenged.

Even before his appointment, Santosh Bhattacharya points out, the CPI(M) had made its intentions of running the university according to its diktats clear. 'In Calcutta University the existing authority, namely the Syndicate, along with the Senate, the Academic Council, etc. were superseded on 14 January 1978 and replaced by a nominated Council which ruled for about four years till another set of bodies were elected under the terms of the new Calcutta University Act of 1979.' The book is replete with many other examples of obstructive tactics used and efforts made to thwart attempts to restore the glory of the university and to improve its functioning academically and administratively.

Outlining the reasons for the Congress's failure to dislodge the Left Front rule for thirty-four years, Pradip Bhattacharya, president of the West Bengal Pradesh Congress Committee said, 'The Congress organization was weak and was unable to fight against the cadre-based CPI(M). Once they came to power through the democratic process, the CPI(M) adopted all Stalinist methods to crush the opposition parties. In the name of '*gana sangathan*' (mass organization) the CPI(M) controlled the police unions and the government employees through their co-ordination committee... The CPI(M) unleashed rampant violence, killing 11,000 Congress workers during its rule for more than three decades. There was total fear psychosis and voters were afraid of going to polling booths. In order to win the elections, the party indulged in violence, capturing booths and rigging the elections. Victory of the CPM was not the victory of democracy but of a Stalinist process,' says Pradip Bhattacharya.

With the victory of the Left Front in election after election, the Congress was demoralized and unable to fight against the organizationally superior election machinery of the CPI(M) with its own weak organization structure. During Indira Gandhi's rule at the centre, particularly under Sanjay Gandhi's influence, New Delhi seriously considered imposition of President's Rule in West Bengal but the idea was dropped after Sanjay's death. The increasing fighting within the Congress made matters worse, according to the Pradesh Congress president. A section of the party was getting restive, primarily the Youth Congress President, Mamata Banerjee. The Congress at the centre was hardly in a position to assert itself, even though the minority government led by Narasimha Rao had managed to complete its tenure (1991-1996).

In many states, governments were formed and fell as a matter of routine but in West Bengal the Left Front was unshakeable, returning to power with unfailing regularity. In 1998, the Congress in West Bengal split into the Congress and the Trinamool Congress but they jointly contested the election in 2001. This gave rise to the expectation in some quarters that there would be an end of the long innings of the Left Front in West Bengal. What lent greater weight to this expectation was Jyoti Basu's decision to relinquish the post of chief minister in 2000 and hand it over to Buddhadeb Bhattacharya, who had been groomed to succeed him and had actually been given the designation of deputy chief minister.

Expectants of a Congress victory were crushed, however, as the Left Front won, although with a slightly decreased majority, 199 seats against 203 in the 1996 elections. Although Jyoti Basu is held responsible for many of the ills of West Bengal including de-industrialization, absence of a work culture and a faulty education policy, and for playing havoc with academic institutions and the collapse of the health system, he is still held in awe nationally, and not only by Communist cadres. It was during his last two terms that he adopted a pragmatic pro-industry approach despite strong opposition from within his party and was responsible for many major industrial projects such as Haldia, Mitsubishi, Bakreswar Thermal Plant etc. It was he who spoke against labour militancy etc. setting the path for Buddhadev to go for industrialization in a big way. He missed being the prime minister by a whisker, when the United Front—a combination of many parties—was in a position to form the government in 1996 and he was requested to take over as the prime minister. He was prevented from doing so by the central committee of his own party, led by Prakash Karat.

Jyoti Basu later called this a 'historic blunder', which the CPI(M) central committee probably realized as well but by then it was too late. Jyoti Basu, with his political craftsmanship and charisma ruled West Bengal from 1977 to 2000, winning successive Assembly elections. As a gentleman, he commanded respect both in the state and the country. The prime minister sought his advice and, in his last years as chief minister, he became a towering figure on the national political stage.

Indeed, Jyoti Basu is a study in contradiction. He was responsible for major failures in administration and development with continuous all round decline in the economic health of the state, but was politically successful. He ruled without interruption for twenty-three years with five successive Assembly election victories; commanded national stature and respect; was invited to be India's prime minister but, finally, retired gracefully with his anointed nominee as chief minister.

The contradictions continued with Buddhadeb Bhattacharya, who was handed the role of chief minister on a platter. He had a clean image, was considered incorruptible, was admired by intellectuals and industrialists alike, hailed as the best chief minister in the country in 2005 by Manmohan Singh and by Wipro chairman Azim Premji as pragmatic and pro-industry, with all leading national industrial houses, led by the Tatas, making a bee-line for the state. Yet he did not survive for more than 10 years. In fact, it is he who presided over the slow disintegration of the CPI(M) and suffered a humiliating defeat at the hands of his arch-rival Mamata Banerjee in the Assembly elections in 2011. I had the opportunity to meet and observe both Jyoti babu and Buddhadeb babu on several occasions and over a long period of time. I found them very different from each other.

Jyoti Basu resigned on account of his failing health and old age on 6 November 2000 at the age of 87 and before the next elections. Instead of being a handicap, this turned out to be a masterstroke for the Left with the incumbent chief minister, Buddhadeb Bhattacharya, entering the election fray with the slogan of a 'New Left'. Actually, the Left Front had been losing ground since the 1990s. There were reports that violence was part of the tactical weaponry used by the CPI(M) to come to power and, once having come to power, to perpetuate its rule.

Some extracts from an article that appeared in *Mainstream* (Volume XLVIII, No 34, 14 August 2010), a journal published from Delhi and founded by pro-Communist Nikhil Chakravarty, are startling. The article was written by D. Bandopadhyay, former revenue secretary of West Bengal who was once considered to be close to the Left and was highly appreciative of the initial successful implementation of land reforms by the Left Front Government. He wrote:

> 'CPI(M) leaders started experimenting with murder as a political instrument way back in 1970, when the party cadres murdered two important Congress leaders belonging to the Sain family of Burdwan town. The level of bestiality that they stooped down to was evident by the fact that they made the mother of the two Sain brothers eat rice drenched with the blood of her two dead sons. As a result, the mother lost her mental balance from which she could not recover till her death a decade later. None of the accused has been punished till date.
>
> 'Devoid of any high ideology and believing in the cult of violence the CPI(M) used murder as a political instrument since 1978 in an organized

> manner…the CPI(M) activists used murder as an instrument of political aggression in the Marichjhapi Island of the Sunderbans… The next remarkable case of mass murder was done on the monks and nuns of the Anand Marg group.'

Bandopadhyay's article goes on:

> 'Thereafter the most significant incident to catch the headlines was the Bantala rape and murder. A senior lady officer of UNICEF and another senior officer of the government of India detected a case of huge embezzlement of UN funds by some CPI(M) organization within the South 24 Parganas district. When they were returning with a lot of incriminating evidence, their vehicle was waylaid at Bantala by the CPI(M) goons. The vehicle was set on fire to destroy all documentary evidence. The driver who tried to protect the two lady officers was killed. Then the lady officers were raped and one of them murdered and her body without any cloth left on the open paddy field. When the then Chief Minister, Jyoti Basu, was informed of the incident, he quipped to the waiting media men: "Such incidents do happen, don't they?" *(Ei rokom to hoyee thake)*.'

Many other such incidents are discussed in the article. Among others, the Suchapur murders where 11 Muslim agricultural workers were killed in a gruesome manner because they demanded that minimum wage rates be fixed by the government from the CPI(M) *jotedars* (landlords). Thereafter, the CPI(M) resorted to political cleansing of territories through murder, rape, arson and loot. Large areas were cleansed of opposition elements by continuous raids, as the British did in the untamed tribal land of the North West Frontier Province. Bandopadhyay's article estimates—on the basis of replies to questions put to ministers in the assembly during the period 1977-2009—that as many as 55,408 murders took place between 1977 and 2009.

Buddhadeb Bhattacharya was inducted into Jyoti Basu's cabinet in

1977 after the Left Front's sweeping victory. In 1982, he lost from the Cossipore Assembly constituency but won again in 1987 after changing his constituency to Jadavpur after which he was taken back into the Cabinet. In September 1993, he was considered the number two man, holding such important portfolios as information and cultural affairs, urban development, municipal affairs. He was well known as Jyoti Basu's blue-eyed boy and tipped to be his successor.

That was when he suddenly resigned from the government on 1 September 1993, openly expressing his ideological differences and criticizing the functioning of the government. He returned on 1 August 1994 just as suddenly as he had left and was immediately re-appointed minister for information and cultural affairs. The inside story of this sudden resignation and equally sudden return has never been told and remains something of a mystery. Some considered it a case of inner contradiction for a dogmatic Communist who was finding it difficult to adjust to parliamentary democracy. Maybe it was a fight between Jyoti Basu's pragmatism and Buddhadeb's dogmatism.

Perhaps Buddhadeb considered that the party was not being true to itself, that perhaps being in power was not really providing any relief to the people and perhaps the party in power was not furthering the establishment of socialism. Chandan Basu's story, appearing in newspapers, may have intensified Buddhadeb's inner struggle. Chandan Basu's forays into business with the support of big Indian and multinational companies were frowned upon and caused many eyebrows to be raised in the party. Media reports alleged that Chandan, being the son of the chief minister, Jyoti Basu, was being unduly favoured by big business houses and Chandan was accused of amassing vast wealth by unfair means.

Buddhadeb Bhattacharya, a new incumbent with a clean image,

was able to lead the party to victory in the 2001 and also the 2006 elections, when the Left Front won with a larger majority of 235 seats compared to 199 in 2001. However, it needs to be noted that Jyoti Basu was a seasoned and hardened politician. From 1940, when he returned from England and joined the party, till 2000—a period of sixty years—he had weathered many a storm. In comparison, Buddhadeb was a relative green horn. He lacked the stature and the maturity of his predecessor.

An interesting incident comes to mind. I had occasion to interact with Buddhadeb Bhattacharya in 1974 as editor of *Caldust*. I was nominated by the All-India Newspaper Editor's Conference (AINEC) in New Delhi to the West Bengal State Government Press Accreditation Committee (PAC). This committee had been dissolved during Siddhartha Sankar Ray's government. Both the AINEC and the All-India Small Newspapers Association took up this issue with the state government, demanding the constitution of the state PAC, but with no result.

I first met Buddhadeb Bhattacharya during the 1967 and 1969 Assembly elections while campaigning for United Front candidates, particularly in the Jorasanko Assembly constituency. When he became information and cultural affairs minister in 1977, I talked to him about the need to constitute the PAC and found him very responsive. However, many months passed with no accreditation committee being constituted and one day I met him at his office to enquire about the latest development. He said that the PAC could not be formed, as there were some problems. This came as a big jolt to me and I asked, a little agitatedly, 'What then is the difference between your Left Front government and the earlier Congress government? Both are the same.' He burst out ferociously that basically we were all Congress people and against the Communist government. 'I do not want to discuss this matter further,' he said dismissively. I was surprised as well as disappointed by his attitude.

The arrogance and intolerance of the government became evident in yet another incident. Our advertisement representative had approached the state government's information department for advertisements. He was told that the editor of the paper should meet Adhir Chakravarty, press advisor to the state government. I knew that no publication could be included in the department's media list without his approval. The director of information had earlier expressed his helplessness: the party had total control over the bureaucracy.

A dhoti-kurta clad tall and lean party man, Adhir babu was soft spoken and polite. He advised me to send him all the copies of *Caldust* for the last three months, which I readily did, assuming that he wanted to verify the regularity of the publication. Not receiving any further response despite having sent him the papers, I met Adhir babu again after a few weeks. When he quizzed me about the editorial policy of our weekly, it became clear to me why he had asked for copies of the paper. Only papers that supported the Left Front government would get advertisements.

'Adhir babu,' I said, 'why did you waste your time and mine by asking for copies of my weekly for the last three months? You could have asked me and I would have told you plainly that although I had actively supported the United Front governments of 1967 and 1969, I am an admirer and supporter of Indira Gandhi.' That was the end of the discussion. Needless to add, *Caldust* never got a single advertisement from the West Bengal government.

It wasn't just with the media; the CPI(M) imposed its will on the Left Front once it secured the dominant position within the Front. The party began to play Big Brother and to ride rough shod over the other partners and even to disregard dissident voices within, including that of the main architect of Operation Barga, Benoy Chowdhury. Thus, while the facade of a coalition of as many as eight parties was maintained till the end, it was the CPI(M) that took all the decisions. Given the personal stature of the chief minister, Jyoti Basu, however, it was possible for him to keep the Front united even though the disdain for other veteran leaders was shocking.

A case in point is that of Nripen Chakravarty. He was one of the builders of the party in Bengal and later built the party in Tripura from scratch. A man of impeccable integrity, who led a Gandhian life even when he became chief minister, Nripen Chakravarty was expelled from the party in 1995 just because, in an interview to a press reporter, he made some critical comments about the manner in which Chandan Basu had been able to amass a considerable amount of wealth. Interestingly enough when, many years later in 2004, Nripen Chakravarty was on his death bed and in a coma, he was readmitted to the party without a word of explanation or apology for his expulsion.

What was happening with the Congress while the CPI(M) crushed every obstacle on its inexorable march forward? All this while Mamata Banerjee was quietly growing in stature, taking the battle to the Left Front camp and paying the price as Left supporters physically assaulted and injured her. Never one to mince words, she even declared that the BJP was 'not untouchable'. The PCC president and Congress strongman Somen Mitra opposed and denounced this statement. Mamata took an aggressive stance calling certain Congress leaders '*tarbooz*' (watermelon)—green from outside and red from within—implying their secret links with Red Communists. 'In general, people believed in Mamata,' said Pradip Bhattacharyya who did not deny, however, that certain Congress MLAs depended on the Left Front for their electoral victories.

'Mamata's charges carried conviction,' he said. Ironically, today both Somen Mitra and Subrata Mukherjee, who were leaders of the Congress at the time of split, are with Mamata Banerjee. Asked about the general impression that the Congress high command in Delhi was not very keen on disturbing the Left Front in the state, Pradip Bhattacharya strongly disagreed, saying that 'the Congress central leadership never advised us not to oppose the CPI(M).' Even during the term of the UPA-1 government at the centre, which had the support of the Left Front, the state Congress opposed many policies and programmes of the Left Front government in the state: 'I personally went to Nandigram and Singur to oppose the Left Front policies and to protect the interests of the farmers but people did not trust us, they believed in Mamata,' said Pradip babu. The TMC was thus clearly emerging as an alternative to the Left Front.

The Communists, however, were, experiencing yet another interesting phenomenon; a new culture. The CPI(M) was splitting people into two categories: '*amader lok*' (our people) and '*amader lok na*' (not our people). Understandably the anti-Congress feeling was deep, with memories of the frenzied political violence during Congress rule from 1972 to 1977 when thousands of CPI(M) cadres lived in the shadows, chased and hounded by the police and the ruling Congress forever fresh in the party's mind. This attitude of dividing the whole population of West Bengal into 'us' and 'them' was developed into a fine art during the thirty-four years of Left rule. The attitude was that 'if you are not with us, you are against us and can expect no help', not even the support that a government is constitutionally bound to give to all its citizens.

That despite its poor record in the matter of governance the Left Front managed to win election after election was something that surprised those who observed the political scene from a distance. Within the state and even outside though, to those who tried to understand and study developments in West Bengal, it was becoming clear that the Left Front had lost popular support and that there were two factors responsible for its repeated successes. For the first three elections, the party was able to draw upon the goodwill created by earlier struggles and sacrifices of the Left leaders. After that the disenchantment with the performance of the peoples' representatives started growing and the earlier regard for the Left turned into distrust and dissatisfaction.

The second factor, paralyzing that section of the electorate who was keen to see an end to the rule of the Left, was the absence of a viable alternative. The Congress leaders, who had virtually capitulated to the Left in return for the loaves and fishes offered to them—mainly in the form of putting up weak candidates helping them to win elections, allotting land plots, getting their children admitted in Medical Colleges under CM quota, etc.—had become incapable of leading the growing anti-CPI(M) forces in the country. Mamata and her Trinamool Congress were gradually emerging, but the snooty middle class refused to accept that someone from the lower middle class, with a poor command of English, could be the chief minister of West Bengal, which had seen stalwarts like Bidhan Chandra Roy, Siddhartha Sankar Ray and Jyoti Basu as chief ministers.

The Left Front lost nearly 6 per cent of its overall support base in the Lok Sabha elections in 2009 to the combined opposition. This was not a case of alliance arithmetic overcoming the collective strength of the Left but a steadfast and major erosion of support, what any psephologist would term a huge swing, caused by a polarization between the opposition and the ruling Front. This polarization ensured that in the civic elections even the Congress did much worse than it did in the Lok Sabha elections, meaning that the Congress was only riding piggyback on the anti-LF polarization led by the TMC in the Lok Sabha elections.

That takes us to the crucial question: why has the Left Front's core base, which has given it years of popular support, deserted it? The answer is not too difficult to find but is certainly uncomfortable. Over the past few years, there has been a steady erosion in the class orientation of the Left Front government in terms of its policies and in the manner in which the CPI(M) has organized itself in many parts of the state. There is a distinctive shift in policy, predicated on the need to industrialize through big-ticket, capital-intensive investment, barely mindful of the consequences of this drive. This drift towards neoliberalism has steadily corroded its pro-poor image. The symptoms were all the more visible in the process of land acquisition—in Nandigram for example—which erupted in a decidedly reactionary and violent manner.

The answer is visible in the manner in which local leaders of the CPI(M) have entrenched themselves and how working class organizations and trade union fronts in quite a few areas have been steadily reduced to agencies led by unscrupulous contractors. Combined with a distinct lack of a pro-active Leftist political imagination on the question of development, the enabling processes of big-ticket investment were seen as inevitable even while emphasis on social welfare and other pressing necessities was lacking. Those wanting to benefit from the ethos of neoliberalism have entrenched themselves in the leadership of the Left Front at various levels. In essence, one can bluntly assert that the core support base of the CPI(M) and its partners has deserted them.

However, since the Lok Sabha poll debacle, Left leaders did work hard to regain the confidence of the Left Front's support base. They stopped all controversial land acquisition initiatives, put greater emphasis on social welfare, implemented the Ranganath Mishra Committee's recommendations on affirmative action for backward Muslims, spruced up the NREGA programme implementation, which had been laggardly in the past and focused on the urban employment guarantee programme, amongst others. The government did try to get back on track.

Yet, without weeding out those entrenched careerist elements who benefited most from the neoliberal drive; without showing a genuine urge to change from within, or even managing to remind the electorate about earlier achievements and focusing more on a negative campaign targeting the opposition, the Left Front simply could not get its message through. There was also the high-handedness of the cadres to contend with. The urban middle classes simply withdrew their support. It is going to be a Herculean task to regain the support of this group, as well as the urban poor and to convince the rural poor, for whom the industrialization drive meant only a loss of land with no assured employment.

After the Lok Sabha election results, one stream of thought believed that the losses were a consequence of the Left withdrawing support from the Congress-led UPA government over the nuclear deal issue. According to this stream, the attempt to build a rag-tag third front coalition just prior to the elections in opposition to both the Congress and the BJP was a political move that was resented and therefore rejected by the people of Bengal. This move ultimately resulted in an alliance between the Trinamool and the Congress and affected the Left Front's electoral fortunes. However, the civic election results were a rebuff to such an erroneous theory.

The post-election review of the central committee of the CPI(M) held on 11-12 June 2011 in Hyderabad cited the 'ganging-up of disparate political forces ranging from the extreme right to the Maoists under TMC to isolate and weaken the Left Front', as one of the causes. The central leadership, in an effort to put the blame at the door of the state leadership, stated in the review that, 'There were shortcomings and weaknesses in some of the policies and measures adopted for the welfare of the people. The mistake with regard to Singur and Nandigram proved costly.'

The review report adopted by the CPI(M)'s central committee was a clear indictment of the state party bosses. The CPI(M) boss, Prakash Karat, was more forthright in putting blame on the state leadership, saying, 'The Left Front could not recover the lost ground in the past two years as much as we expected. It was a big defeat for the Left Front. This has come as a major disappointment. The people have decisively opted for change and given a sweeping victory to the TMC combine.'(*People's Democracy*, 22 May 2011). Earlier, in a joint press statement on 13 May 2011 in Kolkata, Biman and Buddhadeb merely said, 'This result was unexpected. The Left Front accepts the people's verdict and promises to perform the role of a responsible and constructive opposition in the State Assembly.'

A member of the CPI(M)'s state committee, who chose to remain anonymous, furiously lashed out against the party's central leadership. He made derogatory remarks against it, particularly against Prakash Karat, criticizing the party's decision to withdraw support from the UPA government and the expulsion of Somnath Chatterjee. He categorically blamed the party's central leadership for the poll debacle in West Bengal. It has to be said, however, that any attempt to ask for a no-holds-barred collaboration with the Congress effectively reduces the ability of the Left Front to speak and work for the classes that it represents. It stunts, for example, the ability of the Front to portray its differences with the Congress on public policy and on issues of political economy.

The collaboration, in many ways, also resulted in a debilitating double-speak: oppose the liberalization, privatization and globalization policies on principle but implement them in West Bengal nonetheless. It thus reduced the Left's ability to strike up popular alliances with other thriving social movements against rampant neoliberalism. In many cases across India, the CPI(M) was isolated and unable to lead popular movements against unpopular special economic zone (SEZ) projects, because of the incidents in Nandigram. Towards the closing years, this became even more apparent during the Singur-Nandigram episodes that drove the last nail in the coffin of the Left Front government.

Green in the Ascendant

I met a traveller from an antique land
Who said: 'Two vast and trunkless legs of stone
Stand in the desert. Near them on the sand,
Half sunk, a shattered visage lies, whose frown,
And wrinkled lip, and sneer of cold command
Tell that its sculptor well those passions read
Which yet survive stamped on these lifeless things,
The hand that mocked them and the heart that fed.
And on the pedestal these words appear—
"My name is Ozymandias, king of kings.
Look on my works, ye Mighty and despair!"
Nothing beside remains. Round the decay
Of that colossal wreck, boundless and bare
The lone and level sands stretch far away.

—Percy Bysshe Shelley, *Ozymandias*

In 2001, following the first election after Jyoti Basu relinquished his post, Chief Minister Buddhadeb Bhattacharya was somewhat cautious. He was still feeling his way and testing the waters. Although the Left Front had won, there was, for the first time since the Left Front came to power in 1977, a declining trend in public support and number of seats. As against 203 in the 1996 elections, the Left won only 199, while the Congress had almost doubled its tally from 43 to 82. Five years later, the long-term trend of continued dominance of the Left Front was back. In the

2006 elections, the Left Front was victorious with a larger majority, winning 235 seats while the Congress-TMC combine was reduced to 58, compared to 86 in the earlier elections.

At the centre too it was advantage Left Front. Even though the UPA, led by the Congress, had emerged as the largest combination, defeating the BJP-led NDA, which had been in power with Atal Bihari Vajpayee as the Prime Minister, it did not have the necessary majority. It secured only 218 seats (276 are required to cross the half-way mark) and was able to form the government only with the support of other parties, the largest of them being the Left Front with over 60 seats. Sonia Gandhi, president of the largest party and leader of the UPA, decided to stand down and declined to be the prime minister, giving the post to Manmohan Singh who had been the finance minister in the Narasimha Rao government in the 1990s and who was credited with introducing the policies of liberalization and privatization at that time.

The massive victory of the Left Front in the 2006 polls and the fact that the strength of the TMC-Congress combine had declined compared to the earlier 2001 elections convinced Buddhadeb Bhattacharya that this was a mandate for his policy of giving primacy to industrialization over agriculture even though their election manifesto had said that development of agriculture and industry would go side by side. His determination to go ahead with rapid industrialization was further strengthened because the UPA government in Delhi had become dependent on the support of the Left in the Lok Sabha and the West Bengal chief minister expected to get extra support for his bid to industrialize.

With the Left Front thus secure, he and Biman Bose, chairman of the Left Front in West Bengal and secretary of the state unit of the CPI(M), made provocative speeches saying that the central government was now fully at their mercy and they could pull it down whenever they wished to do so. The chief minister also felt that he could go all out to woo private capital, Indian as well as foreign, to bring in investment. Industrialists vied for his attention. Chambers of commerce and foreign business delegations were dropping in one after another. Here was a chief minister of a Communist-led government, who was openly declaring that socialism was not on their agenda, capitalism was. They never had it so good.

Former senior executive with German MNC Siemens and head of India-German Chamber of Commerce B.G. Roy sums the situation up thus: 'For the first time in many years industry received close co-operation from the West Bengal government. This was mainly due to Chief Minister Buddhadeb Bhattacharya, who could sense business. He would always have time for CEOs visiting India and he would leave a good impression. One German CEO commented after meeting him, "He is not a politician, he is a perfect gentleman. I can do business with him."' On one of the first major German investments, 'Metro Cash and Carry' in the retail sector, B.G. Roy quoted the chief minister as saying, 'There are apprehensions but I have understood. It is not easy to make another understand. It takes time but we will do it.'

The chief minister lost no time after his re-election in 2006 and made a dash to Indonesia to meet one Emil Salim, the head of Salim Industries. The Salim Group is Indonesia's biggest conglomerate with assets in industries and businesses as varied as instant noodles—through Indofood Sukses Makmur, the world's largest instant noodle producer—and flour milling through Bogasari, to real estate. The group has been involved in property development and the leisure industry for around thirty years. Its businesses include hotel and resort development, golf courses, real estates, commercial buildings, shopping centres and industrial estates.

It is ironic that Buddhadeb should have chosen a person who was linked to the anti-Communist Suharto group in Indonesia and who was a staunch follower of the policies of liberalization and privatization, which were being opposed by the CPI(M) publicly in India. What kind of a deal was negotiated with him in Indonesia is not known but media reports indicated that the group would invest thousands of crores in a large number of projects and, importantly, require land to the extent of tens of thousands of hectares. Much of the investment would be in real estate projects such as townships.

The first alarm against the land acquisition that was expected to follow as a result of the deal with the Salim Group was sounded from within the party by Rezzak Molla, a leading member of the CPI(M) in West Bengal and an MLA from the Bhangar area of the South Parganas district in south Bengal. The land in the area was multi-crop fertile land inhabited by small and marginal farmers, mostly Muslims. In fact, much of the agricultural land in West Bengal is cultivated by small and marginal farmers unlike in states like Andhra Pradesh, where large tracts of land are owned by families, who are often able to use advanced techniques of farming, particularly for their cash crops.

Rezzak Molla realized that acquisition of land for Salim's projects would mean the end of the party in that area and an end to his prospects of returning to the Legislative Assembly. He openly came out against forcible acquisition for which he was censured and repeatedly asked to keep quiet. However, as the Singur project took shape, developments in Nandigram exposed the signs of unrest in the farming community all over West Bengal.

On 14 March, the situation in Nandigram, which had been brewing dangerously for many months, spiraled out of control. CPI(M) cadres and a thousand policemen attacked the villagers who were protesting against the state' intention to hand over 10,000 acres of their land to Indonesia's Salim Group to build a special economic zone. The police fired to quell the protestors. According to the police, eleven villagers died; district authorities placed the number at fourteen; senior CPI(M) leaders in the state admitted to nineteen deaths. The locals said that dozens died and several hundred injured. A senior leader of the Revolutionary Socialist Party, a constituent of the Left Front, put the figure at fifty dead. There was talk of many bodies being taken away and buried, adding to both rumour and body count.

The CPI(M)'s arrogance was dented as it came under severe verbal attack. Even then, there was no back-pedalling by the party's leader, Prakash Karat and spokesperson Sitaram Yechury. They disingenuously hinted at Maoist triggers in Nandigram, without once acknowledging the sledgehammer policy of the government in West Bengal. The party had to relent, however. The uproar was so great that a stunned chief minister was forced to apologize and withdraw the state's plans of going ahead with the SEZs.

In New Delhi, the commerce ministry quietly announced an amendment to its earlier SEZ policy: 'The developer (of Special Economic Zones) shall make adequate provision for rehabilitation of the displaced persons as per the relief and rehabilitation policy of the State government.' Concerns over a Nandigram-type situation had flared up and spread westwards; the government of Maharashtra held back clearance for Reliance Industries' mammoth SEZ across Mumbai. Meanwhile, the prime minister, at a meeting of directors general of police from across India in New Delhi, reiterated the point that he had made two-and-a-half years earlier; one that had created such a flutter in urban India: 'Maoism and its manifestations are the country's most challenging internal security threat'.

That pretty much answered the question on several minds: are the Maoists in their last phase or are they even more powerful now?

'I can fight the Naxals but not Naxalism. That has to be done only through development,' said a senior police official engaged in combating Maoists. This almost echoed Charu Mazumdar, who once said, 'Naxalbari has not died and it will never die.'

Interesting developments were taking place in Singur, which were soon to dramatically change West Bengal's political landscape. The state government acquired 997 acres for the Tata's Nano car project. The Nano would be a Rs 100,000 car that would, it was claimed by the Tatas, mark a revolutionary advance in car manufacturing technology. In the first few months after his new term as chief minister, Buddhadeb entered into a deal with the Tatas for certain concessions and incentives to be given to the Tatas for the project.

The contents of the agreement had been kept a secret and once, when the government was about to make the provisions of the agreement public, the Tatas went to court to prevent this, claiming that it would amount to revealing trade secrets. The land asked for was acquired for the project under the Land Acquisition Act of 1894. Enacted in the British period, it was intended for acquiring land for such public purposes as the building of roads, bridges, educational or health institutions.

Although there have been some amendments to the law after independence, the basic provisions and the methods of acquiring land remain the same. Under the Act, the government or the authority acquiring the land decides the extent of compensation to be paid to the farmers. Consultation with the owners of the land is required but their consent is not essential.

Those who opposed the Singur project said that, in acquiring the land, many provisions of the law were not followed. While some farmers accepted the compensation cheques, others did not.

The land earmarked for the project was taken over by the state administration amidst protests and began to be fenced off on 1 December 2006. Mamata Banerjee, who was leading the protest movement and had been prevented from entering Singur by the state police, called a statewide bandh in protest, while legislators belonging to her party went on a rampage. Later, she went on a twenty-five-day fast demanding that land should be returned to the unwilling farmers, those who had refused to accept the compensation cheques.

The fenced-off area was being guarded by CPI(M) cadres in addition to a large contingent of police. It was during this time, on 18 December 2006 that, within the fenced-off area, the body of Tapasi Malik, a teenaged villager who was active in the protests, was found. She had been raped and burnt to death. Attempts were made to cover up, alleging that she had committed suicide because of a failed love affair. Later, a CPI(M) activist, Debu Malik, was arrested and, based on his statement, the CPI(M) zonal committee secretary Suhrid Dutta too was taken into custody by the Central Bureau of Investigation, which was investigating the case.

In 2008, the Tatas withdrew from the project, pleading inability to carry on construction work because of interference by the local people, and shifted it to Gujarat, where it was reportedly offered even better terms. Mamata, who had led the agitation, demanded that out of the land taken over by the Tatas, 400 acres be returned to those farmers who had not accepted the cheques and had not agreed to sell their plots. After taking over as chief minister, her first priority was to return the land to these farmers. While the decision to hand over the land to them has been taken, the matter is in the courts. Meanwhile, the Singur and Nandigram movements have served to comprehensively overturn the socio-political situation on the ground. For the first time, the CPI(M) mass base in the countryside was completely alienated.

Although Saugata Roy regrets the Tata decision to abandon the Nano car project in West Bengal, he blames Buddhadeb Bhattacharya for the Singur fiasco. 'In his arrogance and over-zealousness, Buddha mishandled the situation. The farmers felt that the Left Front government was taking away their land. These farmers, the backbone of the Communists, turned against them and this spelt doom for the Left Front government. Left leaders failed to read the writing on the wall,' he says. The Congress high command always looked at the Left as counter to the BJP, which was the main opponent of the Congress at the national level. It never seriously worked to build up the party at the grass-root level—it had not needed to—and the lack of state-level leadership further contributed to the weakening of the party in the state. During 2004-2009, the CPI(M) was setting the agenda and it was against this background that Mamata emerged as the only bet that could defeat the Left Front. Many Congressmen joined her, explains Saugata.

There is no denying though that the successful manufacture of the world's cheapest car in West Bengal, by a company of such professional standing as the Tatas, would have dramatically changed the industrial landscape and mindsets of big business. What was essential was professional management, which Buddhadeb had no clue about, as he wanted to bulldoze industrialization in; not usher it in. In the process his dreams were shattered and the state's image as an ideal destination for industry was in tatters. Most importantly, the incident represented a breach of trust as far as the CPI(M)'s mass base was concerned.

The agitation in Singur and Nandigram and the brutality with which it was suppressed thus led to the series of debacles faced by the Left Front in the elections to the panchayats in May 2008, to the Lok Sabha in April-May 2009 and finally, to the West Bengal Assembly in April-May 2011. The Nandigram movement deserves a more detailed explanation. A proposal under the SEZ Act for a chemical hub to be set up in the Nayachar island area between the Haldia and Hooghly rivers, was cleared in principle by the central government. However, even before the final approval had come, a notice was issued to the residents of the area about the acquisition of land that was to take place for the project.

The notice was issued by an overzealous CPI(M) leader, Lakshman Seth, chairman of the Haldia Development Authority. This sent alarm bells ringing in the area and the farmers prepared for resistance. On 6 January 2007, a Nandigram-based Bhumi Ucchhed Pratirodh Committee (anti-eviction committee) came into being. The Trinamool Congress, through its MLA in the adjacent constituency, Subhendu Adhikari, the Socialist Unity Center of India (SUCI), the Congress and a comparatively newly-formed regional party, the People's Democratic Conference of India, also extended support.

A team from the National Alliance of People's Movements (NAPM) visited the area as part of an international fact finding mission on the forced eviction of farming communities in the state of West Bengal. It said:

> 'When a mass rally and public meeting was held at Nandigram on December 8 and corner meetings followed till night, amidst a large number of police and central local intelligence officials, it was no doubt an exhibition of strength and confidence, determination and commitment to save the land, water and the agriculture, the rural life but through democratic means. The people expressed lack of faith in the promise of their rehabilitation, knowing well what had happened to those displaced due to coalmines, to industries, to dams, to urban renewal in West Bengal and elsewhere. All the people's organizations and political parties represented on the dais also questioned the uprooting of communities for changed land use, more likely to be real estate development, as was suspected by an author, in an article

in *People's Democracy* in 2006.'

In November 2008, when the chief minister and the union steel minister Ram Vilas Paswan were returning from the site of the proposed Jindal steel plant in Salboni in West Midnapur, a land mine blast hit the convoy. Considering this an attempt to assassinate the chief minister, the police unleashed repression on the villagers in the area of Lalgarh, known as Jangalmahal, largely inhabited by tribals. This gave rise to a massive protest movement led by a peoples' committee against police atrocities in Lalgarh and the entire Jangalmahal area in West Midnapur. The Maoists took advantage of the situation to stage a comeback.

The CPI(M), which had dominated the area prior to the police action, tried to retrieve lost ground as the joint forces of the State and the Centre set up their camps and carried on their operations. To ensure that they were able to re-establish their domination of the region they set up their own armed camps even while denying the presence of these camps. However, in January 2011, when the elections to the state Assembly were around the corner, a gathering of the village people who had been protesting against the CPI(M) camps was fired upon from one of the camps in Netai village. Six or seven villagers were killed and many others were injured. The existence of the CPI(M) camps could now no longer be denied. There was a wave of protests from all shades of opinion in the state. Even the non-CPI(M) partners of the Left Front condemned the incident, leading to further isolation of the Left Front, which explains the complete rout of the party in the 2011 elections.

An article in *The Statesman* by the former state bureaucrat S.M. Murshed on the role of state Governor Gopalkrishna Gandhi in Nandigram is worth reading in its entirety:

'On 13th March, the Governor of West Bengal, Shri Gopalkrishna Gandhi, was in Chennai, where he received credible information to the effect that the police had mobilized a massive force on the outskirts of Nandigram in preparation for storming the village and restoring, it is said, a semblance of government. The police force was reinforced by cadres of the CPM, some of them wearing police uniforms. It was obvious to the Governor that the situation was fraught with dangerous consequences. Accordingly, through his principal secretary, Dilip Rath, he conveyed a warning to the home secretary that the police should observe restraint in its projected venture in Nandigram. Nothing, therefore, happened on the 13th March.

'However, on the 14th March when the Governor was airborne en route to Kolkata and incommunicado, the police went into action, and by the time the Governor reached Kolkata, the action was all but complete. Restraint, as advocated by the Governor, was not observed.

'Estimates vary. But at least 14 people were dead, killed both by police and *other* bullets, with evidence of gory blood trails showing that bodies had been dragged for over a kilometre; and several scores injured, to be removed to Nandigram and Tamluk hospitals and to SSKM hospital in Kolkata. Perhaps the death toll was much higher. Women bore stab as well as bullet wounds. Some women alleged rape.

'Stunned by the "*cold horror*" of the events of the 14th March, the Governor issued a statement lamenting the wanton bloodletting and asserting that the events need not have happened. And he visited the Tamluk Hospital to offer the injured men and women such succour as he could. The chief minister surprisingly did not visit any of the injured or bereaved families; or to issue any condemnation of the bloody deeds.

'The statement of the Governor has been criticized in an orchestrated manner in some circles and journals. Has it dawned upon his critics that he is bound in his gubernatorial duties by an oath to defend, preserve and protect the Constitution and the laws of India?

'The Constitution in its Preamble mentions Human Rights as an article of faith and the Directive Principles enjoin upon the government the duty to protect the human rights of citizens. The Governor was thus bound by his oath of office to defend the human rights of individuals. He is also the head of the local Red Cross by which he is sworn also to lend succour to people affected by civic strife. And in Tamluk he was doing no more than to lend succour to injured persons, whose human rights lay tattered. Where did he stray from the straight and narrow path of rectitude? Where did he fail in his gubernatorial duties? There has been condemnation of the proceedings at Nandigram from the CPM's allies in the Left Front, certain ministers making bold, public utterances. And within the party itself, the ageing patriarch, Jyoti Basu, did not mince words in castigating the government for its handling of the situation. But from the CPM itself, there has been no public word of condemnation of the terror and carnage unleashed by the police and its own cadres. This acquiescence in silence tells its own tale of complicity.

'There has also been condemnation from intellectuals, artists, writers and playwrights, screen and stage actors, film directors et al of the bloody events. Certain personalities returned their awards, received by them for their literary or artistic attainments, to register their protest. The protests were aired in public demonstrations of anguish on the streets of Kolkata, with large segments of the populace joining them.

'A state-wide bandh was called by various political parties on 16th March, and I would presume most Kolkatans view bandhs with considerable distaste. Yet there was a spontaneous upsurge of public angst regarding Nandigram which made the bandh a complete success. And I for one endorsed public opinion.

'Stung by this upsurge of public sentiment of all hues and complexions, at last, on 17th March, the chairman of the Left Front issued a categorical statement to the effect that no land at Nandigram would be compulsorily acquired for any industrial purpose and there would be a phased withdrawal of the police from the scene of its recent rampage.

'The chairman's statement came three days late. If it had been made earlier, innocent lives would not have been lost.

'The Governor's warning was not heeded, possibly under political tutelage. When the situation as it happened at Nandigram was clear to the Governor, it should have been doubly so to the minions of his government. But we have become accustomed, or inured, to a system of supineness in which the distinction between the diktat of *His Master's Voice* and the clear requirement of law is lost. The preservation of self is the all-important religion. As a former bureaucrat, I know of the pressures of the system and how to withstand them. Again as a former bureaucrat, the Governor, Shri Gopalkrishna Gandhi, would know this as well.

'Our argument then brings us inexorably to the conclusion that the doctrine of response at superior may nail one or two political heads. Whose, is not far to seek.

'A point to note in passing is that the CPM prides itself on its secular credentials. But what are they truly like? In Nanur, in Birbhum district, 11 sharecroppers were killed in police firing. They all happened to be Muslims. In Garbeta-Keshpur in Midnapore district, 50 per cent of those similarly killed were Muslims. And now in Nandigram, at least 25 per cent of the dead and injured are Muslims. Perhaps, this is an accident of history.'

Land has always been at the heart of politics in West Bengal. Along with a number of other factors, it brought the Left Front to power and helped to a large extent in ensuring its hold on the state. It is the same land issue that triggered the Red brigade's downfall. In 1978, the Left Front's 'Operation Barga' gave legitimate land titles to share croppers. After twenty-eight years, in 2006, Mamata's indefinite hunger strike against land acquisition for the Tatas' Nano project lasted for twenty-five days and made her the harbinger of a new land reform movement. Even the former chief minister, Jyoti Basu, had by then been able to realize the significance of Mamata's meteoric rise.

Worried about the health of a fasting Mamata, Basu once told a TMC functionary who had gone to meet him at his home, 'Tell Mamata to stay fit to fight the battle later.' Perhaps Basu meant to convey to his party men the message that Mamata was on the right track but the party bosses did not take the hint because of their contempt for Mamata Banerjee. Till the last they had underestimated her ability to bring off what appeared to be an impossible feat: the defeat of a well-entrenched Left Front with its well-oiled election machinery.

The mediation of Mahatma Gandhi's grandson and the Governor of West Bengal, Gopalkrishna Gandhi, gave the CPI(M) another window out of the death-trap but once again it refused to read the writing on the wall. The two-year-old Singur crisis was almost resolved as a land-for-land agreement had been reached at a meeting between Buddhadeb Bhattacharya and Mamata Banerjee, after three days of hard-nosed bargaining. As part of the agreement, the government would return the land of all those farmers who had not been compensated. Most of it was within the premises of the Tata Motors Nano car factory in Singur. Governor Gandhi had brokered the talks between the two sides.

Mamata, in turn, announced the immediate withdrawal of her party's two-year-old agitation on the issue and the fortnight-long sit-in demonstration at the factory site. A committee would be set up to work out the modalities of returning the land within a week during which the government ordered suspension of all construction work in the nearby ancillary units of the car factory. The talks, marked by twists and turns, were again unsettled following a last-minute demand by Mamata, after a consensus was reached earlier, that the land acquired by vendors of ancillary units of the car plant at Singur be returned to farmers as well.

Matters were retrieved from the brink again at the initiative of

Gopalkrishna Gandhi. Retired Justice Chittatosh Mukherjee had been invited earlier by the Governor to help with the Singur negotiations. 'My role in the Singur negotiations was limited to advising the Governor. It was really extraordinary that the Governor took this initiative,' said the highly respected Justice Mukherjee. 'Mr Gandhi was deeply concerned over the developments in Singur. News of the continued blockade of the highway and assault of foreign technicians had greatly perturbed him. The Governor made the lifting of the blockade a condition with Mamata before he entered into any arbitration. Earlier, the Governor had reportedly spoken to Ratan Tata requesting him not to remove the plant and machinery, to which Mr Tata reportedly did not respond positively,' said Justice Mukherjee.

Gopalkrishna Gandhi advised that a 'farm-factory balance' be reached to resolve the Singur impasse. He said, 'Through the Singur discussions, I saw earnest participants showing a rare spirit of accommodation. That spirit needs to be operationalized. Reason can be reasonable, passion dispassionate. I believe, given the will, a solution can still be found in a manner that accords with the law, safeguards the interests of farmers, of the small car factory and, going beyond, help in establishing the farm-factory balance that we so vitally need.' However, Mamata Banerjee and the state government failed to agree on the acreage to be given to farmers to compensate for agricultural land 'forcibly' acquired for the small car project. Mamata was apparently upset over the government offering the farmers a 'mere 70 acres' within the factory site against her demand of 'at least 300 acres'. She found the government's offer 'unacceptable'.

The government had placed a comprehensive package before the opposition chief, saying it would provide 70 acres within the project area to the 'unwilling' farmers, of which 40 acres belonged to the West Bengal Industrial Development Corporation

(WBIDC). The remaining would be given from the main project area. The government asked the opposition to look for the rest of the land, according to their demand, outside the project area. It also agreed to provide an additional 50 per cent of the land price to those whose land had been acquired for the project. In case of an absentee landlord, the government said it would provide 50 per cent of the land price in cash to the registered sharecroppers. It also said it would provide 300 days' wages to unregistered sharecroppers and agricultural labourers.

There was more. The government promised jobs to one member from each of the families who lost land and to build schools, roads and hospitals in and around Singur for 'community development' at its own cost. 'The chief minister was reportedly conciliatory too in one to one discussion but was, it seems, overruled by party hawks,' said Justice Mukherjee. Mamata was not yet on a high curve and was looking for an honourable exit. However, the government also had real apprehension that the Tatas would not agree to release 400 acres of land. The CPI(M) felt that if they conceded to Mamata's demands she would be allowed to steal a march on them and gain politically. In fact, the CPI(M) later lashed out against both the Governor and Justice Mukherjee. 'As the talks failed, Gopal Gandhi was sorry because he genuinely wanted a settlement,' said Chittatosh Mukherjee.

The bottomline was that the failed talks turned out to be a springboard for Mamata, who never looked back. Tata Motors started setting up the unit in Singur, 40 km from Kolkata two years ago to produce the world's cheapest car—the Nano—priced at Rs 1 lakh. The company had invested Rs 1,500 crore in the project, which was essentially built on prime agricultural land, with the local community far from supporting it. Courtesy its thirty-four year rule and successive electoral victories, the Left was blinded to the fact that it would not be able to handle the groundswell of opposition. Nor did it ever believe that its impregnable 'Red Fort' could be captured.

The TMC's loss of control of the Calcutta Municipal Corporation in 2005 and its electoral defeats in the 2006 elections, when the TMC lost more than half of its sitting members, further convinced the Left Front of its invincibility. Mamata Banerjee's challenge was dismissed as that of a 'one-man army'. It was an army that was, however, riding on the anger of a whole community that had been dispossessed over many decades thanks to poor industrialization and inadequate agricultural growth.

Analyzing the lack of industrial development, Chittatosh Mukherjee explained that, 'a disinclination to work and too much opposition' have been a matter of concern in West Bengal. Industrialists have also failed to modernize their industry in the state. 'Mamata's down-to-earth approach appeals to the masses. There is lot of public goodwill behind her. However, she needs good advisers and good administrators... It is in the background of these events that the defeat of the Left Front and the overwhelming victory of the Trinamool-Congress combine needs to be understood,' he explained.

Cocooned in power's ivory tower, the Left Front was fast losing touch with the masses. The writing on the wall had been clear since 2005, indicating a loss of support that was continuing at a steady pace. In the panchayat elections in 2008; in the Lok Sabha elections of 2009, which gave the TMC 19 seats against only nine for the Left Front; in the Kolkata municipal elections in 2010, where the TMC contesting on its own—with the Congress putting up its candidates separately—won 93 seats against 39 for the Left Front and only seven for the Congress: the march of the green brigade was unmistakable. Yet the Left leaders were continuing to wallow in delusion, basking in the glory of past achievements and ignoring the winds of change.

The TMC slogan of '*poriborton*' (change) had caught the imagination of the people. The weight of the incumbency factor was making itself felt. In fact, the people wanted the Left to go without caring for who would take its place. With her cry of *Ma, Mati, Manush* (Mother, Earth and People) the fifty-six-year-old firebrand leader, Mamata Banerjee, had stolen the thunder of the Left and the result was there for all to see. It was to a large extent a negative vote but the people also realized that Mamata was the only alternative in the absence of any other credible opposition. The Congress had lost its anti-Left image. Years of Mamata's cry that the Congress was the CPI(M)'s 'B team' and a tarbooz (water melon) had left its imprint on the minds of the people; more so because it was not far from the truth. The fact that the Congress at the centre had sought and been able to get the support of the Left Front for UPA-1 did not improve matters for the Congress in West Bengal.

Jyoti Basu was a far-sighted politician. In an interview to Karan Thapar in 1999, he made what today looks like a prediction. He was asked, 'The Left has been in power for twenty-two years. How long will this last?' Jyoti Basu, who was then the serving chief minister, replied, laughing aloud, 'I should say forever but I won't... There is no doubt the Left is the best for Bengal but I am not sure if prolonged years in power is the best thing for us. You see power distances a party from its roots. It also makes politicians complacent and perhaps arrogant and worst of all, you end up losing contact with ordinary people and real life. Of course, it won't happen for a while. But when it does my colleagues won't like it. In fact, most of us won't be ready to admit its happening. After being at the top you begin to think you will never fall down.' How right Jyoti Basu was. Most of the Left leaders were 'not ready to admit it is happening,' as predicted by Jyoti Basu. There is no enemy like ego and pride.

Contrast this with Mamata's consistent refusal to share the platform with Left leaders, particularly with Buddhadeb Bhattacharya, rejecting several truce offers. She was very particular about not being seen sitting beside Buddhadeb even at the meeting convened by Gopalkrishna Gandhi at Raj Bhavan to mediate on the land dispute in Singur. She made leader of the opposition Partha Chatterjee sit next to the chief minister, while she herself occupied a distant corner seat avoiding both physical proximity and any eye contact with him. From the viewpoint of the '*bhadralok*' this was uncivilized conduct, not in consonance with the norms of parliamentary democracy. However, it bolstered her image among her core supporters, who were dead opposed to the CPI(M) and harboured feelings of hatred towards the Communists. She knew that only this strategy would establish her and her party as a genuine alternative to the CPI(M). Her language may not have been very diplomatic but it suited the taste of her constituents.

Political violence has always been at the core of politics in Bengal even in the pre-independence era. As one has seen, the origin of the Maoist movement, considered today to be the biggest internal threat by Manmohan Singh, can be traced to the Naxalism of the 1960s in West Bengal. Mamata knew well that she needed street fighters more than political rhetoric to face and confront the CPI(M) cadres. In Nandigram, she reportedly used the tacit support of the Maoists for this purpose. Mamata could read the telling signs of the Left Front having been pushed to the brink and wanted to ensure that in the 2011 polls they would be pushed out. In the Lok Sabha polls of 2009, which followed the peasant movements in Bhangor, Singur, Nandigram and Katwa, the CPI(M) lost 22 seats out of 24 in the districts of North and South 24 Parganas, Howrah, West Midnapore, Bankura and Purulia, once considered to be CPI(M) strongholds.

In a last-ditch effort to retain power the Left Front played the old card of a 'New Left' with new faces. Nine ministers and 80 sitting MLAs were dropped by the CPI(M) and the Left Front as a whole fielded 150 new candidates but the move was too little and too late. The panic in the ranks was apparent but the party bosses refused to believe that they could be voted out. The Left leaders loudly declared that the Left Front would form its successive 8th Left Front government in the state. 'We will form the government, maybe with a reduced majority', was the refrain of Left leaders.

With the Left's defeat on the horizon, a section of Congress leaders, who were not necessarily anti-Mamata but die-hard Congressmen, were deeply concerned about the post-election fate of the Congress in the state. For them the sweeping victory of the TMC meant the doom of their party in West Bengal, as in Tamil Nadu. This section, believed to be close to the AICC leadership, while working for the defeat of the CPI(M) also wanted to cut the TMC to size, denying it a single party majority. The CPI(M) leadership was approached by this section of Congressmen with a list of 42 constituencies, seeking their support to win these Assembly seats.

A personal experience is worth recalling here. I was sitting in the chamber of the Speaker of the Assembly Hashim Abdul Halim, surrounded by a few Left leaders. The first two phases of the 2011 Assembly elections were over. Asked about their prospects, I said that, 'there seems to be a pro-*poriborton* wave and the Left Front may be reduced to around 100 seats.' This statement was greeted with loud protests: 'Do you think the Left will lose more than 100 seats? This is a canard spread by the business community.' I explained, 'According to my information, the business community is generally with the Left Front as it has developed a cozy relationship with it over the years. It finds Mamata unpredictable and considers her an unknown entity.'

Meanwhile, one CPI(M) candidate entered the chamber; the

election in his constituency was over. On being asked about his prospects, he said, 'I have won the seat in the last three elections and my last margin was over 10,000 votes. I will win but margin may be reduced.' He did not sound very confident and made an interesting observation, 'This time the voters, even those I have known for years, are silent. They are not talking; it worries me.' Eventually it proved to be a silent revolution. The voters were clever and did not want to disclose their hand as they felt that an open stand would expose them to reprisals after the election.

During the discussion, I found Hashim Abdul Halim's stand most perplexing. On most occasions I had found him giving frank assessments, sometimes even at variance with the party's stand during private discussions. Many of my journalist friends and political leaders, cutting across party affiliations, will vouch for this. On this occasion, he strongly agreed with his comrades that the Left would form the government, however with a reduced majority. This was in contrast with his views expressed in a similar discussion a few weeks earlier with some friends, including myself, when he had said that the Left Front might not return to power.

Hashim Abdul Halim had then also said that this would be good for the party. He was deeply cut up over the party's central committee's decision to expel Somnath Chatterjee and withdraw support from the Congress-led UPA-1 government. To be fair to the Speaker, despite the expulsion he never severed his relations with Somnath babu and continued to maintain official as well as personal relations with him. When the West Bengal Legislative Assembly was unveiling the portrait of Jyoti Basu at the Assembly house, Halim proposed the name of Somnath Chatterjee to do the unveiling and sought the permission of the CPI(M) bosses in Delhi. Seeing the changing mood and the declining influence of the party, Prakash Karat was left with no alternative other than to agree.

However, in a post-election interview, Halim candidly accepted that he had known that the Left Front would lose the Assembly elections. 'The party had made certain mistakes, including those at Singur and Nandigram. Midnapore district was left in the hands of Lakshman Seth, who was very unpopular. The mafia had infiltrated the party ranks and, despite several discussions within the party, the rot could not be stemmed as it had acquired very deep roots at district and local levels. Money was playing a big role in the party. The delivery system was faulty. The policy of offering employment to party men was wrong as it antagonized a large number of unemployed both within and outside the party. Hence the introduction of employment only through the Public Service Commission or the School Service Commission was a step in the right direction by the government to correct this malady. In Singur, an arrogant party chose not to take the peasants into their confidence. This would never have happened had Jyoti Basu been the chief minister,'observed Halim.

The Forward Bloc leader Ashok Ghosh was equally frank.'Despite our strongly expressed protests both in public and in private about Singur and Nandigram, the CPI(M) never agreed to correct its policy.' Octogenarian Ashok babu boldly admitted, 'It was our fault that due to greed for power and perks, we did not withdraw from the government. We should have withdrawn long back. In fact our party state council had decided to contest the panchayat elections singly, not jointly with Left Front but could not follow it up because of opposition from our ranks.'

Mamata had deliberately followed a policy of keeping a safe distance from the CPI(M) leaders. Many found this strange, some even termed it uncivilized in parliamentary democracy, but Mamata was playing according to a well-orchestrated plan that, as subsequent events proved, paid her handsome dividends. She was aware that most Congress leaders had fallen victim to Jyoti Basu's charms.

Most of the state Congress leaders had, after a long period of Left rule, reconciled to the Left's invincibility and had lost all hopes of gaining power. Jyoti Basu knew that Congress leaders, accustomed to power and positions, could not remain without perks and privileges for long. The CPI(M) used this weakness selectively by offering many posts and positions, including the party's support during the elections. Many Congressmen were known as Jyoti babu's blue-eyed boys and it was an open secret that some Congress leaders depended on the CPI(M)'s support for retaining their Assembly seats.

It is against this background that Mamata's order to Trinamool leaders to keep away from Left leaders has to be understood. She and her party were offshoots of the Congress and she knew her party men only too well. She had been at the receiving end of violence and attacks by the Left on her life, and betrayal and expulsion by her own senior colleagues in the parent party. This made her suspicious, particularly of those Congress leaders who had oscillated between extending and withdrawing their support to her. During her days in the Congress, Indira Gandhi had been Mamata's idol, and she has tried to emulate her at all times. She has a deep sense of insecurity, and does not trust anybody. Nor is she not averse to splits in the party or to cobbling together strange alliances. Like Indira Gandhi, she appeals to and connects with the masses over the head of the party and draws her strength from the people. The party needs her; she does not need the party. Mamata, like Indira, has an inherent dislike and contempt for intellectuals and armchair politicians.

Mamata Banerjee is also comfortable with street fighters and lower-rung leaders. She does not believe in having equals in the party. Despite being made the offer of more than one cabinet post in Manmohan Singh's council of ministers in UPA-2, she declined. In her scheme of things, there was no space for any Trinamool leader to be equal to her in protocol or in status. Dinesh Trivedi was appointed cabinet minister for railways only after Mamata gave up the post and she was left with no alternative; a concession that she later withdrew under compelling circumstances.

Mamata has, however, greatly matured in politics in recent years. She is less mercurial and more pragmatic, though her intolerance for opposition breaks out often enough. Most of the former senior Congress leaders, now in Trinamool for their political survival, are given posts and positions but have neither political clout nor are held in high regard. She knows that, as with Indira Gandhi, they may be the first to bail out if and when Mamata's boat starts sinking. She remembers that many Indira loyalists, including Siddhartha Sankar Ray, who was her main adviser during the Emergency, were the first to denounce Indira Gandhi after she lost the elections in 1977.

Mamata has been very careful and selective in her attacks on political leaders. The contrast in her approach towards the two chief ministers, Jyoti Basu and Buddhadeb Bhattacharya, has been striking. Jyoti babu was not considerate towards Mamata when she was attacking the government and carrying on her agitation. Mamata faced brutal attacks on her person from Jyoti Basu's police but she never made derogatory comments about Jyoti Basu or slighted him publicly. In fact, she was courteous and respectful both during his term and thereafter. This was reciprocated by Jyoti babu on critical occasions. Mamata showed no such consideration for Buddhadeb. In fact, she missed no opportunity to make humiliating and sarcastic remarks against Buddhadeb Bhattacharya.

Her changed attitude towards Somnath Chatterjee after his expulsion from the CPI(M) also reflected Mamata's growing political maturity. Young and unknown, Mamata's political career had begun with her stunning and unexpected victory in the Lok

Sabha election in 1984 against a three-term heavyweight member of parliament, Somnath Chatterjee, and that too from a constituency, Jadavpur, which was a stronghold of the party. Despite Somnath babu's campaigning for selected CPI(M) candidates in the 2011 Assembly elections against Mamata's nominees, she responded with the gesture of sending her senior leader, Partha Chatterjee, to his house after the election. Since the 2009 Lok Sabha polls, Mamata has been trying to play her political cards well, making new friends, carefully avoiding making new enemies but not always succeeding.

Power is a cementing force but power also attracts and promotes defection. Mamata knew that given the poor prospects of the Trinamool coming to power, it would be difficult to keep her flock together. Any defection could weaken her party. This was a difficult task, given the successive Left victories. A Trinamool MLA from Jorasanko, who had won in 2006, was in a great hurry to become a minister. In no mood to wait for five years till the next election, he had entertained the idea of trying his luck with the Left Front and started courting some of its leaders. In the process, he accepted the chairmanship of a legislative committee, which did not go well with Mamata. The Left wanted him to resign from the party and also from the Assembly seat in order to embarrass and jolt the Trinamool. They even promised him a nomination and a ministerial berth if he won.

The 'if' worried the MLA, who was looking for a way to avoid another election and also to escape anti-defection laws. A cat and mouse game ensued. Mamata, fully aware of the goings on, kept her cool, refused to expel him, waiting till the 2011 elections to punish him by refusing to re-nominate him from the same sure seat. Unlike the Mamata of the 1970s and 1980s though, she did not even rebuke him, leave alone expel him. She merely expressed her inability to offer him the seat and requested him to campaign for the party, assuring him that he would be suitably rewarded in due course, which she did by offering him the chairmanship of a state corporation.

Then there is the mercurial Mamata temper that often gets the better of her. She has suffered politically and damaged her image because of her impulsive outbursts. As a fighter she believes in shouting her opponents down. However, she has acquired the acuity and resilience of a mass leader even while retaining and exhibiting her inner contradictions. She has matured a lot, despite her inability to shed her hysterics and histrionics, which are unbecoming in a new-age leader.

Yet, Mamata is trying to be a politician. She snubs the WBPCC president—Indira Gandhi style—but waits for the AICC interlocutor to take his chair before her. She makes caustic remarks against Biman and Buddha and in the same breath and pays regards to veteran Forward Bloc leader Ashok Ghosh, even indirectly complimenting Buddha's cabinet colleague, the PWD minister and RSP leader Kshiti Goswami. Her winning over of quite a few pro-Left intellectuals, writers and artists and neutralizing some of them was nothing short of a coup, enhancing her image dramatically in the pre-election period. For Mamata the biggest favour was conferred by CPI(M) boss Prakash Karat, when he expelled *bhadralok* Somnath Chatterjee who was highly regarded by middle class, educated Bengalis and then withdrawing support from the Congress-led UPA-1 government at the centre.

'Different parties in the Left Front have analyzed the causes for the defeat of the Left Front in 2011 Assembly Polls differently,' observed Ashok Ghosh. The only surviving founder of the Left Front was remarkably frank in his assessment: 'The CPI(M) is mainly responsible for the present situation. Its class character was destroyed. We failed to recognize our main enemy. The CPI(M)-CPI consider the Congress to be a progressive bourgeois party and ranks the BJP as the main enemy. Remember, in 1977, it was the CPI aligning with the Congress and it was the CPI(M) later on supporting the Congress. Buddhadeb's contention that capitalism has not fully developed spelt doom,' explained Ghosh.

Political circles in West Bengal have been perplexed by the relationship between Ashok Ghosh and Mamata Banerjee. Ashok babu blew hot and cold while talking about Mamata and her party. On the one hand, he described the TMC as a one-woman party with no party, no cadres. On the other, in his assessment, Mamata may emerge as a nucleus for forging a third front not only in the state but also at the centre. Asked about his personal equation with Mamata, the longest serving general secretary of the Forward Bloc smiled and said, 'She respects me and keeps calling on me.'

Kiranmoy Nanda, a minister in the Left Front government and a socialist leader, said that smaller constituents of the Left Front had no say in policy formulations and their opposition to policies in Nandigram and Singur were overlooked, 'although our party was dominant in the district'. Nanda, who lost the election, was so disillusioned with the Left Front that he actively involved himself with Samajwadi Party activities in Uttar Pradesh. Mulayam Singh Yadav not only appointed him as a party general secretary but also nominated Nanda to the Rajya Sabha after the Samajwadi Party's grand victory in the Uttar Pradesh elections. For Mulayam, Nanda is a conduit to Mamata in the context of national politics. That much was evident during the joint press conference held by Mulayam and Mamata announcing their choice for presidential candidates.

The Left Front is held responsible for the Bengal's de-industrialization and lowering of standards of such revered institutions of higher learning as Presidency College. As far as the work ethic in the state is concerned, the best joke comes from the halls of the Indian

Coffee House, the renowned meeting place of the city's intellectuals and students: if revolution struck Bengal after 5 pm, government employees would demand overtime to participate! The decline of the Left has been obvious for many years even at the national level. Its erstwhile dominance of the trade union movement is also ebbing with the BJP's Bharatiya Mazdoor Sangh (BMS) as the leading trade union organization, followed by the Congress-backed INTUC.

Even Somnath Chatterjee, former Speaker of the Indian Parliament, recently remarked, 'My agony is that the Left parties are becoming more and more irrelevant. The space occupied by the Left is shrinking; it is time for some change. One is not sure if the failure of the CPI(M) is at the organizational or the governance level but there is certainly a growing distance between the people and the party. There is smugness in the leadership. There is arrogance,' he said in an interview to *Outlook*.

The banishment of the Left in the 2011 elections to the West Bengal Assembly has been a massive blow to those democratic and progressive forces in the country that considered West Bengal as a bastion of the Left. Yet after thirty-four years of Left Front government and its seeming invincibility, its own mass base voted it out of office. Some general features of the verdict stand out. The people decisively opted for change and gave a sweeping victory to the TMC combine. There was a total consolidation of all the anti-Left forces, ranging from the right to the Maoists on the extreme Left. It is also evident that the Left Front could not recover the ground lost in the past two years on account of political bungling and administrative overreach.

Analysing the defeat of the Left Front, Hashim Abdul Halim said, 'The lack of credible opposition led to arrogance among the party leaders. Mamata emerged not only as an alternative to the CPI(M) but to the Congress with its continuous decline. After the

Left's withdrawal of support from the UPA, Sonia Gandhi's one-point programme was to defeat the CPI(M), which facilitated the Congress-TMC alliance. The Left certainly wanted the Congress to survive. There was deep resentment in the middle class about the anti-Bengali attitude of the central CPI(M) leadership after what happened first to Jyoti Basu, denying him prime ministership, and later on to Somnath Chatterjee with his expulsion. Somnath Chatterjee should have been allowed to run Parliament as per Parliamentary norms. The party should not have tried to run Parliament.

'The Left Front could have lost even in 2006 had the Congress and Mamata been together. The difference in the polled votes was less than 1 per cent—0.98 to be specific. I had warned the party and particularly told Chief Minister Buddhadeb Bhattacharya not to make such boastful comments that "we are 235". That was a case of misplaced confidence,' Halim observed.

Even though the Left Front garnered an additional 11 lakh votes in 2011 compared to the 2009 Lok Sabha polls, there was a reduction of 2.2 percentage points in the vote share compared to the Lok Sabha polls. Their prolonged period in government led to the aggregation of negative factors. The defeat in West Bengal has led to a barrage of allegations against the CPI(M) and the Left. The results are being portrayed as a catastrophe from which the CPI(M) will not be able to recover. Another line of attack pursued by some commentators is to pronounce the ideology of the Communist Party anachronistic and the electoral verdict as the end of the relevance of socialism and Marxism worldwide.

Prakash Karat believes differently. 'That these may not be correct assertions can be understood by the fact that the fall of the Soviet Union had no material impact on the CPI(M). In fact, in the 1990s, the party grew and became stronger, both in West Bengal and Kerala. As far as ideology is concerned, the CPI(M) draws on the theory and practice of Marxism by creatively applying it to Indian conditions. This is not a static position but one that evolves constantly. Those who are writing the epitaph of the CPI(M) and the Left Front in West Bengal overlook the fact that even in this defeat the Left Front has polled 41 per cent of the votes. Over one crore ninety-five lakh (19.5 million) people have voted for and supported the Left Front. The loss of such a Left-led government is a setback but it cannot be seen as a permanent and fundamental loss.'

Perhaps the Left is trapped in its own jargon. Claiming to be the social conscience of the country and supposedly committed to the welfare of the downtrodden and underprivileged sections of society, the leftists have ironically performed poorly in their own states as far as the spirit of the welfare state and development indices go. In contrast, rightist parties like the BJP or socialists like Nitish Kumar have done comparatively better on social welfare programmes. The ideas represented by the Left in India has also been questioned by senior BJP leader Murli Manohar Joshi. 'If concern for the poor defines the Left, Deendayal Upadhyaya and Indira Gandhi were Leftist too,' Joshi has said.

The Left leaders have never learned to accept criticism and are seen as people who only talk to each other. I faced this on many occasions. You are welcome as long as you speak their language but even a mild suggestion contrary to their stand will draw loud protests. Till the night before their defeat in West Bengal, CPI(M) leaders believed that they would scrape through. After my round of visits in the city of Kolkata on the day of the elections, I mentioned my apprehension about the likely defeat of Buddhadeb Bhattacharya to a CPI(M) leader who reacted violently, calling me an anarchist and Mamata's stooge. The CPI(M) was so divorced from reality that, four days before the election results, in an exclusive interview Buddhadeb Bhattacharya told *Outlook* (9 May

2011), 'We have realized our mistakes. We had lost touch with people at the ground level but we have re-established it. We are confident that we will have a comfortable majority.'

When Buddhadeb was going all out to woo industry, he did not pause to ponder upon the lesson that S.M. Krishna had learnt in Karnataka or Chandrababu Naidu in Andhra Pradesh. His aggressive pro-industry stance alienated him and his party from his core group of peasant and working class supporters. Jyoti babu would keep the best of personal relations with industrialists but his pro-labour image always remained intact. He was also careful while making pro-industry statements. He would say, 'I will have to make friends with industrialists, as I want investment here. I cannot tell them to get out of the state because we are Communists.' Buddha's stance did considerable damage to the party when he said, 'According to classical Marxism there is a fundamental rift between capital and labour but here we are practicing policies of capitalism not socialism. We do not want to raise slogans like "*ladai, ladai, ladai chai*" (fight, fight and fight) and close down factories.' The government was not only seen to be pro-rich but also against the poor, which was a cardinal sin. However, the fact remains that it was Buddhadeb who, despite resistance from within the party, continued with his efforts to improve the industrial climate in the state, wooing investors and earning the confidence and support of Manmohan Singh's government at the centre.

Ma, Mati, Manush

> The history of the world is full of men and women who rose to leadership by sheer force of self confidence, bravery and tenacity.
>
> —Mahatma Gandhi

> Blessed is he who expects nothing, for he shall never be disappointed.
>
> —Alexander Pope

Even as the news of the CPI(M)-led Left Front's mauling at the hands of Mamata Banerjee's Trinamool Congress was splashed all over on the historic Friday of 13 May 2011, the larger question about the future of the TMC government and the state lurked in the background. The overwhelming emotion was euphoria on the streets of West Bengal; it was spontaneous and joyful, reckoning that the hour of change and transition ('*poriborton*') had come. The slogan of 'Ma, Mati, Manush' had touched a chord in hearts and minds but it also meant that Mamata had a pledge to fulfill. Understandably, in the midst of celebrations and expectations were voices of apprehension and caution.

From Writers' Building to the coffee houses, the questions were: Will Mamata be able to redeem her pledge of a renaissance? Will industries flock to West Bengal given Mamata Banerjee's impetuous image, post Singur and Nandigram? Can she convince farmers who have voted for her that she has a more benign land acquisition policy? Will the Trinamool Congress's disconcerting proximity to the Maoists cast its shadow over the state's law and order? Could an insistent Mamata weigh down the UPA government with her demands for the state? Will there be an outbreak of violence between entrenched Left cadres and enthusiastic TMC party workers? How long will the honeymoon between the Congress and the TMC continue? Will the Left pay her back in the same coin—that of playing cussedly obstructionist politics? Above all, how long will the Mamata government survive?

Expectations in Bengal match the enormity of her victory: an enabling environment, law and order, physical infrastructure *(bijli-sadak-pani)*, delivery on social infrastructure (education and health) and an efficient and corruption-free administration. Given the sheer size of the agenda and the complexities around delivering on promises, many political observers and analysts were reluctant to give Mamata a full five-year term.

Coming after such a massive victory, this assessment confused many but did not surprise an astrologer, Kartick Kalyani Chatterjee, considered close to TMC leaders who had correctly predicted the outcome before the elections. 'The TMC will win with a thumping majority. Mamata may decide not to become a chief minister. Even with her as chief minister the government will not last for more than two or three years. The Left Front will not come back to power between 2016 and 2019. The interim elections will favour the Congress,' pronounced Chatterjee. Whether the forecast was based simply on planetary positions or reflected the widespread unexplainable apprehension of many in the state is difficult to say.

Former Speaker Hashim Abdul Halim's take on the survival of Mamata's government was different, though. 'The Mamata government should survive its mandated five years. However, it will depend on her performance and also on how we in the Left Front re-organize ourselves. So far there have been only announcements and promises, no performance... Mamata opposed FDI in retail because the Left opposed it. It was tactical, not ideological opposition. The Mamata government has not given any relief in local sales tax to reduce the burden of the people due to the hike in petrol prices. There is only lip service. The Left Front government had reduced the taxes,' he pointed out to me a few months after the elections.

Mamata's most significant success has been in ensuring almost total peace in the state in the post-election period. There was no evidence of political vendetta and violence as the new chief minister reconfirmed her pre-poll commitment of 'not revenge but change'. The process of political consultation and dialogue with the opposition, absent during the Left Front's rule, has been noticeable. Her personal honesty, apparent sincerity, courage and determination will hold the key to sustained popularity. She has also shown unexpected maturity in dealing with many administrative and political issues. Clearly, she means well and wants to do many good things to many people. Clearly, she is also a political leader in a different mould and people would like to believe her pre-poll assurance that she will 'bring in democracy not party-cracy'. She has begun well.

'Mamata is a tenacious person but her administrative capability is yet to be established. Her performance as the railway minister was not up to mark. Moreover, she has never completed her tenure as a central minister. The erosion in her vote bank has started. We will bide our time. New faces in the party will emerge. The party congress will decide about the future course of action. In the Assembly most of the rules are being violated. New Bills are not being sent to the Standing Committee as per rules. No importance is being accorded to the opposition as there is no big opposition and also because of the undemocratic character of the leadership. All these will cause their downfall. However, the future of Bengal is bright and the future of the Left is brighter. A stronger Left will emerge,' Halim said. Asked about his personal equation with Mamata, he said, 'It is good: I was at her oath-taking ceremony and was invited to the Assembly House at a ceremony to unveil the portrait of the late Siddhartha Sankar Ray. Mamata came to my home when my daughter passed away,' he recalled.

There is no doubt in Mamata Banerjee's mind, as she said in her election manifesto, that her task is to refashion West Bengal. That can only begin by dismantling the legacy of the Left Front.

One aspect of the legacy has been this: there has been an alarmingly steep decline of Bengal in terms of industrial production. From the commanding position of having a fifth share of ex-factory value of industrial output in India, it is now struggling to maintain a 4 per cent share with an almost vanishing profile of manufacturing industries. Indifference towards the building of infrastructure has put the state in the 17th position and in terms of social indices, in the 10th position amongst all Indian states. Bengal has fallen behind in almost every aspect of physical infrastructure: roads, communication, ports and electricity distribution. Governance and the creation of both physical and social infrastructure is the first priority and challenge for Mamata Banerjee's government. Are the right signals emanating from Writers' Building? On the industry front, the signals so far seem to be somewhat confusing at best and this upsets people who welcomed her advent at the helm of affairs in the state in 2011 with soaring expectations.

The fact is that Mamata Banerjee has promised almost everything: the moon on a silver platter. Yet it would be churlish to question her ways at this juncture; even the much-vaunted '*poriborton*' will take time. 'It would not be realistic or justified to take a view of the quality of Mamata's administration within this short period,' feels Bikram Sarkar, former bureaucrat and Trinamool MP.

'For the past many years, the bureaucracy and political leadership have been working under one political party in power. By and large, the bureaucracy tends to forget its role as civil servants, which is neutrality and fair play for all people. This, unfortunately, happens because there are poor leadership qualities in the bureaucracy on the one hand and the overbearing attitude of the political parties, literally gobbling up the entire administration, on the other,' said Sarkar.

'There were many instances where people could not have an FIR registered with the police unless it was cleared by the local secretary of the party in power. Justice was denied for a long time. The main function of the bureaucracy is to advise their political bosses without fear or favour. There are many instances of bureaucrats failing to serve in this way,' says the former MP. He should know, being an IAS officer and having served as commerce and industry secretary during the Left's rule.

The Trinamool Congress' election manifesto set a 200-day short-term and a 1,000-day long-term target for rejuvenating the industrial scenario. The 1,000-day programme in the manifesto is more like a wish list than a proper action plan. Mamata Banerjee is yet to present a comprehensive package of policies for developing the state. People know what she is against but no one has a clue about what she is for. Her anti-industry image, which has stuck to her ever since her opposition to the Tata Motors plant in Singur, is not helping matters. Much more is needed on the ground than verbal enthusiasm and attractive phraseology.

This state of uncertainty affects diplomatic feedback from the state too. A senior Japanese diplomat told me recently, 'We are not clear about the West Bengal government's industrial policy. We are, therefore, unable to explain to our industry back home the comparative advantage and disadvantages with other states like

Tamil Nadu and Gujarat. We have good assurances but no clarity. Investment follows industrial policy; not vice-versa.'

Managing expectations, managing infrastructure, managing finances, managing work culture, managing political contradictions within the state—from the ultras to separatists—and, finally managing her image are competing priorities for Mamata Banerjee. These translate into progress with agriculture, primary health, consumer markets, primary education, governance, infrastructure, investment and the macro economy. While achieving this complex agenda will take time, stakeholders are known to be impatient as confidence turns to questions. In the absence of any major policy announcement, it is no surprise that there has been no big-ticket investment announcement. The most visible change remains the new street lights in Kolkata, while most investment proposals talked of by the chief minister are from the government or public sector undertakings, which have not inspired confidence thus far.

Such diffidence notwithstanding, the change of guard has certainly ignited a fresh bout of optimism in the state that demands that the chief minister take personal initiative to make dreams come alive. Beginning with measures to change the extremely negative image of the state as slothful, with a poor work culture and an anti-capital attitude to industry, a supportive policy regime and a strong social commitment is needed. Yet this is not just a matter of managing the state's image; it is actually changing the character of the state. This transcends the business of beautification and branding that, important as they are, cannot attract investment in a country where states compete for investment from domestic and international investors.

In a world where funds are scarce, the states that win offer very real benefits. Branding helps this process, as is evident in the case of Gujarat, which has achieved a spectacular turnaround, like a phoenix rising from the ashes of communal disrepute to become a magnet for investments. West Bengal needs to bring about genuine change and project that it has indeed achieved that change. There is, of course, a great deal of misrepresentation about the state that needs to be corrected through professional communications. Though late in the day, the Left Front government had embarked on a brand-building mission by engaging the globally known Saffron Consultants. It needs to be reiterated that brand consultants must, however, be given 'brandable' material to work on; one can hardly create a brand out of thin air.

Mamata is, of course, the biggest brand that the state currently has. Her biggest asset is her indomitable spirit and uprightness. She is also a lady in a hurry and wants to do a great many things, fast and in a strikingly different way. She is not shy of taking innovative, imaginative and ingenious steps such as her plans to revive Legislative Council, the appointment of parliamentary secretaries for the first time in West Bengal and the appointment of a mentor group for Presidency College. Her first days in office were refreshingly different. Her firm orders to police to act independently and fairly and to take action even against her own party workers saved the state from inevitable post-election violence and bloodshed. Her agreement with the Gorkha Janmukti Morcha and firm handling of the Maoist problem in Jangalmahal are important gains showing her political leadership and maturity. So far, Mamata and the Maoists had worked together to fight their common enemy CPI(M). After the elections, however, Mamata took firm administrative and police action to curb continued violence.

Forward Bloc leader Ashok Ghosh says, 'Mamata has a dual character. At one point of time Mamata and the Maoists were working on a political understanding with the Forward Bloc,

RSP and SUC, with the CPI(M) as the main enemy. The CPI(M) has also been divided over how to deal with Mamata on different issues. Jyoti Basu and his followers pursued a policy of having a working arrangement with the TMC while the hardliners, led by the Buddhadeb-Biman combine, opposed it. Currently, we are in a laboratory. Although we are still with the Left Front, we are looking at different options. The TMC may emerge as the centre point for forging a third front both locally and nationally.'

Governance and building physical and social infrastructure remains a stupendous challenge. Mamata Banerjee's initial visits to government hospitals to shake up the health bureaucracy must have convinced her that the disease is much deeper and that no cosmetic surgery would help. The state-run hospitals have a long way to go to deliver good quality, prompt and humane services to patients. Similarly, it will not be easy to brush the cobwebs off the administrative apparatus and put things back on track. Even Jyoti Basu had failed to ensure discipline among state government employees and enforce attendance on time at Writers' Building. He had to succumb to the pressure of the CPI(M)-controlled coordination committee.

In her move to save the state's premier educational institutions and bring back the glory of yesteryears, Mamata seems to have taken the right route. She appointed a mentor group of academicians and educationists to select and guide vice-chancellors giving more freedom to academic councils. If she persists, she may indeed give the state's educational institutions freedom from political interference and party apparatchiks. Mamata's decision, despite her promise in the party manifesto, to defer the creation of an Upper House in the West Bengal Legislative Assembly also shows her growing pragmatism. She took into account the opposition of the left and, more importantly, the huge financial burden that it would impose. Power sometimes makes one a rapid learner.

The most important lesson Mamata is learning is coping with empty coffers. For thirty-four years the Left presided over the state's decline. Industry fled from the state, farm growth tapered off and money was scarce. The TMC-Congress combine is largely dependent on a special financial package from the centre, which has chosen to lecture the state on managing its finances before loosening the purse strings. If West Bengal is to scale up its economic activity and development it will have to take—and deal with the consequences of—tough and unpopular options. Given the political situation and with a large number of opposition-ruled states also clamouring for financial favours, it may not be possible for the Congress-ruled centre to go out of its way to sanction a package for West Bengal. Meanwhile, the centre's lukewarm response to Mamata's demand for a big financial package to bail out Bengal is wearing out the chief minister's patience.

Financial management apart, land (*mati*)—which has brought Mamata to power—will be the other big problem. Without a credible land bank, industry will shy away. While this is a problem common to the whole of India, a very adverse man-land ratio, fragmented land holdings and politically disastrous land acquisition strategies make this problem particularly severe in West Bengal. Land is proving to be the most difficult issue for Mamata in her daunting task of industrialization. 'The solution lies in identifying land where industry can be set up without displacing people and disturbing traditional agricultural livelihood,' says Saugata Roy, MP (TMC), union minister of state for urban development. The proposed land acquisition bill, if implemented, will push up the cost of projects manifold. Mamata's stand so far of not intervening in land acquisition for private industry is proving to be a severe setback to industrial, infrastructure and urbanization projects.

The search for solutions has not always thrown out the right one. Business chambers have found themselves saddled with a government circular asking them to provide details of the land allotted, used and surplus land available with all their members. Chambers believe that this information should be available with the government departments and that the government should write to companies directly on this sensitive issue. Clearly, the state is trying to identify unused land but there may be better ways to do so. There is a need for constructive dialogue between land sellers and buyers to overcome land-based conflicts in order to achieve equitable growth.

Recent developments in Jangalmahal and the inevitable confrontation with the Maoists will make it more difficult for Mamata to make any big concession on her declared land policy of no government role in acquiring land for private industry. Many state governments, including Maharashtra and Gujarat, have opposed the centre's proposed land acquisition bill, which stipulates that the purchase price of land has to be at least six times the current market price and the consent of 80 per cent of those affected by the project is to be obtained before acquiring a piece of land. This process of land purchase can carry on indefinitely and, with exponential rises in the cost of land, the projects will become unviable. Even with public sector projects that have been announced in the state, with central audit agencies watching closely, it may not be feasible for such companies to buy different pieces of land at different prices, which is inevitable in the process of direct purchase of land.

Yet, for Mamata Banerjee the challenge is to not repeat her predecessor Buddhadeb Bhattacharya's mistakes, while keeping his momentum for the state's industrialization intact. The other facet of this problem is to improve knowledge-based skills in the state. Despite the acknowledged intelligence of the average Bengali, the state has failed to train it in keeping with the knowledge-based growth paradigm. Not just the IT sector, even manufacturing needs different skills today; without a substantial growth in manufacturing, the employment scenario will not improve; without new skills manufacturing will find it difficult to take root.

These are inherited problems for the new chief minister. After demolishing the industrial environment for decades the Left Front realized by the dawn of the 21st century that, in a liberalized economy, there is no alternative to industrialization to ensure rapid economic growth and face the challenges of rising unemployment among educated youth. By then, however, enough damage had been done. The state's image was dented. Existing business houses reluctant to invest further were shifting and expanding elsewhere. Pan-Indian industrial houses were shy to invest in Bengal, referring to its hostile industrial environment. Buddhadeb started well but messed up on land issues by attempting to forcibly bring in industry against the voices of locals and agriculturists.

Mamata's reaching out to business and industry by having regular interactive meetings has been highly appreciated and many misgivings about Mamata's anti-industry image have been removed. Her decision to direct industry minister Partha Chatterjee to hold fortnightly meetings with the captains of all leading Chambers of Commerce has also been a unique step to overcome the trust deficit between the government, business and civil society. Yet, in the absence of a clear-cut stand to support industry's quest for land, the cluster meetings have failed to achieve anything significant as yet.

The president of a leading business chamber commented, 'Meetings are gradually becoming routine, with no concrete results. Any discussion on land is anathema to the government and the "single window clearance plan" is also facing hurdles.' Another regular participant remarked, 'It is now becoming a mere formality. Meetings are convened at odd hours at short notices; no major hopes survive.' The only tangible result so far for the state has been that the government has persuaded a few chambers to donate ambulances. A small fund-starved chamber has 'resented' the request of the government but, left with no option, it is busy collecting extra funds from its members.

The common perception is that India is governed from New Delhi. In reality, the state capitals have begun to matter more. In his blame game it was Jyoti Basu's common refrain of that 'we are in a federal government, our state has a limited power', passing all the blame on to New Delhi, partly to cover up his government's failure and partly to lower expectations. After the abolition of the licence-permit raj in 1991, there has been a need for massive investment and effective delivery in terms of physical and social infrastructure, mainly in education and health and transformation of agriculture. In all of these, the states are key actors. It is up to states to design effective implementation strategies. Maharashtra and Gujarat have expectedly excelled but even states like Bihar and Chhattisgarh, both under non-Congress governments, have registered double-digit growth in 2010-2011 at 14 per cent and 11.5 per cent, respectively, against the national average of only 8 per cent. The better-governed states can certainly push the bar and improve welfare measures for their people even within a federal structure.

The recent Assembly elections results in Bengal show that at the ballot box, more than anything else, it is governance that matters. A leading businessman and president of the Bharat Chamber of Commerce, Ashok Aikat, says that the new government in West Bengal should first drop the 'blame-the-centre' theme invented by Jyoti Basu thirty years ago, as this has actually harmed the state immensely. Advocating hard and even unpopular measures to shore up the state's economy, Ashok Aikat says, 'The lack of real economic development has shrunk the taxation base, resulting in an ever-increasing budget deficit. As there is a limit to what the centre can provide under a federal budget, the new government is required to take decisions that may not be populist to increase resources. Delaying tough decisions for long is neither good economics nor good politics as the window of opportunity fades very fast.' Erstwhile union finance minister Pranab Mukherjee had issued a warning against borrowing: 'Bengal has piled up a staggering public debt of Rs 2.03 lakh crore. So, more borrowings will not do. The state must step up its revenue earnings.' Mamata, who had been banking on Delhi to bail her out, has so far refused to raise taxes or tariffs, a populist policy that is not appreciated by Manmohan Singh.

The contrast between Mamata Banerjee and Jyoti Basu is clear in the way the latter cynically managed expectations. While Mamata has raised huge expectations; Jyoti Basu survived on managing and tempering them: 'Ours is not the government of India. As state government, we have limited powers and resources and are trying our best to ameliorate the sufferings of the poor people of the state to the best of our ability.' Mamata, in contrast, has been liberal with promises and assurances with such declarations as: 'Kolkata will be London and Darjeeling will be Switzerland'. She has also announced some railways and PSU projects, saying, 'This is our Diwali gift for the people of West Bengal… Industrial revolution is coming to the state.' However, the sceptics are not convinced.

Mamata's strategy to browbeat the centre while bargaining for a deal seems to have misfired: she threatens, but does not talk. Manmohan Singh has Himalayan patience while Mamata's patience is running out because she needs the centre's financial support to deliver on her promises. She has no other option. The centre needs Mamata's political support but has other political options to compensate for the loss of her 19 Members of Parliament. Mamata's strategy of 'raising voice and showing eyes' is neither good economics nor good politics.

Her most critical failure has been in arriving at a viable fiscal plan to bail the state out of a deficit of over Rs 2 lakh crore. Mamata's petulant bargaining style has yielded mere piecemeal benefits. 'She is forever sulking that the prime minister is not listening to her,' says political analyst and veteran journalist Tarun Ganguly, a pre-election supporter of Mamata Banerjee. The electorate is getting increasingly impatient. Summing up its attitude Ganguly says, 'We do not want to know all that. How do you do it is your business. We want results.'

Her recent refusal to accompany the prime minister to Dhaka and her open disagreement on the river water sharing issue turned out to be a 'diplomatic humiliation' which left Manmohan Singh red-faced. In turn, the prime minister rebuffed Mamata in his inimitable way on her threat to withdraw support from the coalition government at the centre on the petrol price hike issue, calling her bluff by refusing to roll back prices. To add to that, the state level leadership of both the Trinamool and the Congress are at loggerheads on a daily basis.

The decision of the Congress central leadership to forge an alliance with the TMC at any cost in the 2009 Lok Sabha polls was to 'teach the CPI(M) a lesson for withdrawing its support and also to enable it to form the UPA-2 government. It was a compromise on unreasonable terms but dictated by circumstances, with the Congress having no alternative,' says Om Prakash Mishra, general secretary and spokesperson of the West Bengal Pradesh Congress Committee. He is happy about the 2011 Assembly poll outcome with the Left Front finally defeated, but takes a pragmatic view. 'Although the terms of alliance with the TMC were one-sided and against the interests of the Congress, the party agreed to them because people wanted change. The Left had to be defeated and that would not be possible without a Congress-TMC alliance. It is also an accepted fact that the TMC's credibility as an anti-Left force was more credible than that of the Congress. It was a correct decision.'

Om Prakash Mishra, however, did not spare the TMC for splitting Congress votes in 1998. 'The TMC should get the credit for keeping the Left Front in power by splitting the Congress votes in 1998. There was an upsurge in the Congress then; it secured 46 per cent of votes in 1998.' His take on the survival of the Mamata government is perplexing, though. 'The TMC may complete its five years' term but with a different composition.' Discounting any possibility of elections ahead of 2016, he added a caveat: 'It depends on the run-up to the polls.' Meanwhile, the relationship between the TMC and the Congress is not good and is unlikely to improve in the future. 'In fact, it may turn worse,' says Mishra. 'The Congress high command listens and appreciates the views of the state Congress leadership but will not take any decision that will force the TMC to go to the opposite camp.'

What about the future of the Congress itself in West Bengal? 'We are entering a different political era in the state. The days of the thirty-four year rule are gone. Political alignments will change more quickly than expected. Ultimately it will be triangular scenarios with the CPI(M) vs Congress vs TMC. The Left Front will disintegrate and new political equations will emerge,' Om Prakash Mishra explains. As far as the performance of the Mamata government is concerned, 'It is a huge relief that the Left Front is out of power. That itself is a big relief for the state. Mamata's extraordinary zeal gives some hope but so far there is no correlation between promise and performance.' He was not too concerned about the deteriorating relations between the Congress and the TMC. 'We may contest the 2013 panchayat elections separately but both will gain in seats and votes at the cost of the Left Front in the short term.'

The UPA's electoral standing, meanwhile, is slipping dramatically. To go by the *India Today*-ORG Mood of the Nation 2012 survey, if a general election were to be held around February 2012, the Congress would have got around 110 seats, its lowest ever tally. In mid-2009, it got 206 seats. The NDA has nudged ahead. The BJP would have improved its tally from 116 seats in the 2009 general election to around 140 seats in February 2012. The non-UPA and non-NDA parties seem to be the real gainers of the Congress' decline. For the first time since 1996 neither of the two leading alliances, the UPA and NDA, would be anywhere close to the majority mark of 272 in the Lok Sabha. In a nutshell, the next Parliament could see a prime minister from neither the Congress nor BJP. This is where Mamata's strategy of a third front, both in the state and the centre, becomes relevant. Ashok Ghosh of the Forward Bloc confirms this. Mamata's eyes are already on the prime minister's seat. Interestingly, she was the third highest rated chief minister in the country, after Narendra Modi in Gujarat and the pragmatic Nitish Kumar in Bihar, an improvement from her fifth position in August 2011.

The fact is that Mamata and the Congress can hardly ever be allies: one can grow only at the other's cost. Both parties have the same background, the same ideology and seek to occupy the same space. The alliance has been one of convenience. Mamata's mistrust of the Congress, both of the state and central leadership, is no secret. Many late entrants from the Congress into her party do not truly enjoy her confidence. The mistrust is mutual. One need not be a rocket scientist to realize that even during the 2011 Assembly elections, there were Congress leaders who were working to ensure that Mamata's Trinamool did not secure an absolute majority but remained dependent on the Congress's support for the majority. Mamata's mistrust is thus well placed.

Driven by the need to engage in the politics of convenience and despite getting an absolute majority, the Trinamool invited the Congress to join the government. Their objective was to lay claim to the centre's financial support. The Congress too, having been out of power in the state for such a long period, did not wish to miss the opportunity to share power, even as a minority partner. It hoped to keep its cadres together and to deter en bloc defection to the Trinamool, while strengthening the party with the help of the state goverment apparatus.

Politically speaking, the Trinamool and the BJP-led NDA can be natural allies in West Bengal, particularly in the context of the CPI(M) being the main opponent of the TMC in the state. A BJP-led NDA will not have any truck with the CPI(M) whereas, in a given political situation, the Congress will not shy away from seeking or providing support to the CPI(M). They are not untouchable for each other and there is a past history of the one having relied on the support of the other. The strengthening of the TMC in West Bengal is directly at the cost of the Congress whereas the BJP does not feel threatened, either at the centre or the state, by the growing strength of the TMC. Both have different political spaces. Moreover, Mamata, like Nitish Kumar, has the image and capacity to keep her Muslim support base intact, even with an alliance with the BJP-led NDA.

Nor are the BJP and the TMC strangers to each other's ways, having successfully worked together earlier. The TMC's prospects of receiving generous financial support from the NDA rather than from the UPA government are also brighter. A strong TMC will only erode the Congress's position in West Bengal. The Congress at the centre will not be able to seek the support of Left parties as long as the TMC-Congress alliance is alive in West Bengal. The Congress realizes that the Left is a more reliable and less demanding partner than the unpredictable TMC.

With this background of political realities, the TMC should follow a more mature policy of cementing ties with the Congress based on reciprocity and mutual respect. The TMC has the capacity to emerge as a strong regional party with its own organizational and regional strength and to maintain cordial relations with the central government of any party and colour for the benefit of the people of the state. The policy of confrontation with the centre will lead the TMC nowhere. It is governance, economy and welfare that pay electoral dividends, not the politics of convenience or confrontation.

Despite total policy stagnation at the centre, with the UPA being paralyzed by scams, there has been impressive policy dynamism in several states. West Bengal is nowhere amongst the best in any major area in the recent ranking by *India Today*'s State of States series 2011. The anti-incumbency factor did not play any role; as Nitish Kumar, Tarun Gogoi, Raman Singh, Narendra Modi, Naveen Patnaik, Shivraj Chauhan and the Akali Dal in Punjab, representing different political colours, were re-elected in recent examples of successful political management. Clearly, then, the centre of India's political gravity has moved away from the centre to the states over the last two decades; the key being good governance. Electoral and other alliances follow.

Commenting on the Congress-Mamata Assembly poll alliance in 2011, Pradip Bhattacharyya, the Pradesh Congress president, said, 'I cannot say we were unhappy but we should have got more seats, particularly better winnable seats... We sacrificed to fulfill the desire of the people to throw out the discredited Left Front government.' He insisted though that had the Congress fought the elections alone, 'it would have been almost impossible for the TMC to defeat the Left Front, despite the wave in its favour.' Asked about the post-election Mamata-Congress relations, he said candidly, 'I cannot say it is a sweet relationship but I also will not say that it has reached a breaking point.' As far as the survival of the Mamata government is concerned, the Pradesh Congress president believes that, 'the government will survive for five years, with or without the alliance.' Reminded that the Congress had suffered wherever and whenever it had entered into an alliance with a regional party, he was candid. 'Alliances weaken the Congress. The Congress should fight alone,' almost echoing Rahul Gandhi's slogan in the context of the Uttar Pradesh elections in 2012.

Between the promise of change and its fulfillment falls the light of good intentions. Mamata Banerjee pointedly requested the speaker of the Assembly to give 'more importance to the Opposition' and, if necessary, to give the Opposition members more time than to those belonging to the Treasury benches. She highlighted this by saying that the government under her leadership wanted democracy and not party rule. She thus removed the barrier between 'us' and 'them' that had been erected by the previous regime. Her statement immediately created an atmosphere of goodwill. It is now a matter of sustaining this spirit, which is easier said than done.

Nothing alienates the people from a government more than a trust deficit. If Jangalmahal turned away from Buddhadeb Bhattacharya's government and joined the Maoists, it was because the people there no longer trusted the administration. Mamata Banerjee's biggest challenge is to regain the confidence of the people of Jangalmahal and wean them away from the Maoists. It may take her some time to succeed in such a difficult mission. Her decision to retain the central forces in the area for the time being makes good administrative sense. It may have prompted the Maoists and their sympathizers in civil society to cry foul but the state government cannot afford to halt the anti-Maoist operations by central forces in the area until the state's writ is allowed to run there.

It is, however, one thing to announce a generous welfare package and quite another to see its benefits actually reach the people for whom it is meant. Erstwhile programmes were of little consequence because, thanks mainly to political interference and administrative inefficiency, the beneficiaries were not reached. If confidence is to be rebuilt, the government's focus needs to be on implementation. Peace with the Maoists is crucial for Mamata's strategy but its success will depend on how she delivers on her promises, which include return of land in Singur and withdrawal of central security forces. That some impact of her good intentions is being felt in the badlands is clear. The Naxalites are on the backfoot but this is not without complexities.

The handling of the situation in Jangalmahal exposed a deep misjudgment, a tendency to tokenism and, at worst, invited the charge that the TMC had cynically played the 'Maoist' card for electoral gains. Mamata had demanded the withdrawal of joint forces from Lalgarh during the Left Front's rule. As chief minister, instead of acting on that, she called a four-month ceasefire but her efforts to get the rebels to the negotiating table ended in acrimony and much finger pointing. As hostilities duly resumed, the support of the intellectuals that she had won during the agitations in Nandigram and Singur began ebbing. After a planned rally by groups calling for an end to operations failed to find space in Kolkata, author Mahasweta Devi called Mamata's policies 'fascist'.

Trinamool MP Kabir Suman penned songs in honour of rebel leaders. The joint forces' success in eliminating Maoist leader Kishenji was a bit muddied by charges of it being a fake encounter amidst dire predictions of a blow back. Mamata is meeting the image crisis with a mix of tough talk on the Maoist front and resolute attempts to show results, economy-wise. The surrender of some key ultra members and the death of others are significant developments. Kishenji, the towering Maoist leader, would not have died had those people who had protected him for long years not changed sides. It is, however, through development and not by annihilation that peace will be restored. There is no better antidote to the politics of grievance than of development, whether for dealing with terrorists or industrialization.

The basic agenda of the Left Front during the 2001 and 2006 Assembly elections was industrialization. There was nothing wrong with this agenda but the process was questionable. Buddhadeb Bhattacharya had declared unequivocally that 'in a capitalist society, industrialization is needed for development and for industry big capital is required to be mobilized no matter what the source.' Mamata too has no alternative but to go for sustainable industrialization for which she must attract private capital, both Indian and foreign. The government also cannot shy away from participating in the process of procuring land for large-scale industries. Here is a case for out-of-the-box thinking if there ever was one because a dramatic change is needed.

Transforming a state from a laggard to a vibrant one is not easy. It makes little sense to argue that the ouster of Tata Motors has not dented the image of the state. The US Consul-General in Kolkata, Ms Beth A. Payne, was reflecting the views of most Kolkata diplomats when she said, addressing a CII meeting, 'If the Tatas cannot run their business here smoothly, what is the hope for foreign investors? Signed agreements can be rescinded for political reasons and there is a security threat to the working environment and the workmen.' The hopes generated by the election of a new government have to be translated into reality.

India is a young nation with some 65 per cent of its 1.2 billion people under the age of 35. Youth is officially defined as those between the ages of 13 and 35. Approximately 460 million people fall in to this category and it is this segment that must deliver for India to reap the 'demographic dividend'. Yet the youth is hardly happy in India; it is angry with the country's political classes. The response to Anna Hazare's movement provided a glimpse of this anger. That said, India's young still have faith in the country's democracy and electoral systems. They are optimistic and believe that they will enjoy a better life in terms of education, freedom, income and lifestyle, than the previous generation.

There are two expectations that this group has from the government: governance and transparency, because both the politician and politics are treated with suspicion. Today's youth is decidedly more materialistic, better informed, more ambitious and more confident in this post-Ambassador car era. A survey conducted by Coca-Cola reveals that the Indian youth across cities and villages said its main ambition is to 'become rich'. The boy from Bihar wishes to become 'Billgay' (Bill Gates). That is true of the youth of Bengal too.

What has Mamata done to ensure that these dreams come true? Eminent journalist and former editor of *The Statesman*, Sunanda K. Datta-Ray, observed in his column in *The Telegraph* six months after the Trinamool assumed power that, 'there is still little evidence of a comprehensive overall strategy that goes beyond populist declarations of intent. In the race for the chief ministership, Ms Banerjee showed herself as a person with a vision. As chief minister, she has yet to demonstrate that she has the ability to turn vision into reality.'

Even a seasoned analyst like Tarun Ganguly is disillusioned with the 'abysmal' performance of the new government as far as governance is concerned. 'If the morning is any indication of the day, things do not look good at all,' he says. Ganguly says that the editor of a Bengali daily, whose newspaper had backed Mamata before the Assembly polls, has now earned her wrath for criticizing it. 'I am as much in their bad books today as I was in their good books before the elections,' he says, adding that, 'the future of Bengal does not look bright at all. We are doomed because we have no choice.' Ganguly is not the sole prophet of doom.

Even so, this play of perceptions does not explain all the doomsday talk. At its root is a series of decisions and indecisions, actions and inactions that betray the new government's tendency to adopt policies detrimental to progress. Compounding Bengal's perilous fiscal deficit problem is the government's refusal to increase revenues. In response to Mamata's demand for a bailout—including her suggestion for a moratorium on interest payments to the centre—the prime minister suggested that she mop up revenue by raising the price of electricity. Mamata refused. She may be coming around to the inevitability of increasing tariffs, however.

'Such populism is ultimately going to backfire. Even the Left Front had discarded these measures in the 1980s. The new government is adopting them and repeating their mistakes,' says Ganguly. Indeed, consumers are not happy with the downside of cheap electricity: Bengal has gone back to the era of power cuts. Strengthening the impression of easy populism was, of course, the TMCs belligerent opposition to FDI in retail, which many perceive as regressive. State finance minister Amit Mitra, who advocated it when he was with FICCI, now finds himself in the uncomfortable position of having to rationalize a U-turn.

The state's economic woes are only one part of the spectrum, where the sheer enormity of the ailment can perhaps be seen as an attenuating factor. It is in the arena of politics proper that Mamata is finding it hard to stave off the impression of being rather less skillful than she promised. A willingness to look for amicable, pro-people solutions to the Maoist problem in Jangalmahal and the Gorkhaland dispute in the north had been big items on the TMC's calling card before the elections. Of these, there is a semblance of success as far as Gorkhaland is concerned, though in a strictly qualified sense. The state, centre and the Gorkha Janmukti Morcha did enter into a tripartite pact but the Gorkhas have by no means given up their demand for a separate state. In fact, they see the pact as validation and a sign of incremental progress.

For many, raising expectations sky high was a strategic error committed by the chief minister and has prompted searching questions. That these are being asked within 365 days of coming to power—normally considered a 'honeymoon' period for any new government—indicates erosion of hopes. To tide the disaffection in other areas, Mamata has launched her public relations initiative: a 10 per cent of dearness allowance arrears to state employees for starters. Even admirers say that 'Didi' has raised very high hopes that the dream of *Sonar Bangla* (Golden Bengal) is just round the corner. Partha Chatterjee, her close aide and industries minister, says, 'The people of Bengal want nothing short of a miracle. They believe Mamata Banerjee will twirl a magic wand and every wrong will be set right,' particularly on the employment and industrialization front.

Apart from an eroded industrial base, what is Mamata's industrial inheritance? Looking back at the industrial development in West Bengal, particularly since independence, the state has continued to be largely dependent on tea, jute and engineering industries, promoted and developed by the British. Many tea gardens and jute mills were taken over by Marwari business houses. Many are now languishing from neglect, no modernization and little fresh investment. Most celebrated engineering firms of yesteryear are either closed or have been taken over by the government. One of the few non-Raj green-field automobile plants, Hindustan Motors, is sick, with its heavy machinery division having been shifted to Tamil Nadu long ago. Major business houses have either declined or have shifted elsewhere.

'Industrialists have left Bengal, leaving behind only the traders and promoters,' say sceptics who have a fair understanding of the state. Most of the so-called big businessmen in Kolkata were order-suppliers or petty traders not very long ago. Western, southern and even northern India hosts the real hubs of major industrial houses—recording rapid growth. Of the Birlas, who started from Calcutta, the eldest, ninety-four-year old Basant Kumar Birla, lives in retirement here but his forty-four-year old grandson Kumar Mangalam, chairman of the Aditya Birla Group, who took over reins of the Rs 3,000-crore group in 1995, is now worth Rs 1,50,000 crore and lives in Mumbai. This is true of all the business houses: the Birlas, Singhanias and even the Jindals. Everywhere the story is the same; everyone has quit the state to prosper elsewhere.

There are deeper issues, other than economics, that are also responsible for the absence of a pro-industry environment in the state. A lack of local entrepreneurship has created a social divide with most of the business and industry being owned by communities of non-Bengali origin. In this cultural capital of India, poverty is traditionally respected and wealth is frowned upon. Businessmen are considered dishonest and a class of exploiters, immoral and unethical. They neither command respect, nor a voice in governance.

The relationship between the government and business has been adversarial, with the Tata episode not helping matters. The 'blame the centre' attitude of the successive state governments, almost since independence, has not helped but, unfortunately, continues in various confrontational ways. Significantly, for decades chief ministers of other states have been taking delegations to different states to invite and seek investments on a regular basis. The chief ministers of West Bengal, since B.C. Roy's time, have considered it below their dignity to do so. Ego, pride and a sense of superiority prevent them. While Jyoti Basu made friends with industry, it was

Buddhadeb Bhattacharya who dramatically changed his approach to business and industry. Given his friendly relationship with the prime minister and the central government, he was largely successful in attracting both Indian and foreign investment and in creating a pro-business environment. Buddhadeb, however, went overboard because he misread the desires of his vote bank. They wanted jobs but not at the cost of their current and confirmed source of livelihood.

There is little doubt that Bengal has to be a part of the India 'rising' or 'shining' story. India's growth achievements are indeed quite remarkable. Per capita income has grown at a compound rate of close to 5 per cent per year in real terms between 1990–91 and 2009–2010. The GDP growth rate was 7.8 per cent during the 10th Plan period (2002–03 to 2006–07) and GDP growth for 11th Plan period has been 9.30 per cent for (2007-08), 6.70 per cent (2008-09), 8.40 per cent (2009-10), 8.39 per cent (2010-11) and 6.88 per cent in 2011-12.). These are no doubt exceptional growth rates, the second highest in the world, behind China. The fact remains though that 'the progress of living standards for the masses, as opposed to a favoured minority, has been dreadfully slow—so slow that India's social indicators are still abysmal', as Nobel Laureate Amartya Sen points out.

There is no denying that there has been a failure to ensure that rapid growth translates into better living conditions for the poor and this is true especially for Bengal. Broad-based social progress can only be achieved by correcting the neglect of elementary education, healthcare, social security and related issues and prioritizing policies for inclusive growth. Many states have achieved all this through democratic engagements. Kerala, Tamil Nadu and Himachal Pradesh have the best social indicators among all major Indian states. A simple index of children's health, education and nutrition clearly places these three states at the top. Despite wide historical, cultural and political differences, they have converged towards a similar approach to social policy and the results are much the same too. There is a crucial lesson here for West Bengal.

Mamata Banerjee evokes both hope and apprehensions as chief minister. To describe her as 'unpredictable' would perhaps be an understatement. She danced atop Jaiprakash Narayan's car as a young Congress worker; grabbed the collars of several politicians to make her point; announced her resignation from the Narasimha Rao government at a public rally at Brigade Parade Ground; hurled her resignation at the Lok Sabha Deputy Speaker because Somnath Chatterjee refused her adjournment motion; declined to accompany Prime Minister Manmohan Singh to Dhaka at the last moment, opposing the Teesta Treaty; threatened to withdraw support from the UPA government on the petrol price hike and suddenly withdrew the threat; and, finally, pulled the rug from under her own party man and railway minister because he had dared to raise railway fares. She has worked hard to deserve the description of whimsical.

As long as Mamata was a lone ranger no one took her seriously. The first manifestation of the trust of the people in her came in the 2008 panchayat polls when the TMC first routed the Left Front from East Midnapore and South 24 Parganas areas. This was followed by her grand success in the 2009 Lok Sabha polls and, finally, her victory in the 2011 Assembly polls. Mamata had scored a hattrick for the TMC. Given her fiery temperament, her intransigence on issues and her ambivalence, a senior leader from her own party candidly admitted, 'She is a highly emotional person who is totally ruled by the heart.'

The TMC is a non-conventional party. So is its leader. Everything depends on her whims and fancies and no one dares disobey her orders. Hierarchy begins and ends with her. Yet, it is the only party that after splitting from Congress has not only survived but even overtaken parent party electorally emerging as the main party. A party functionary, on the condition of anonymity, said, 'Rs 2 crore is needed everyday to feed the party machinery. Nobody knows how it is collected, but there is no dearth of funds.' Mamata is known for her honesty and no businessman can claim close proximity to her. Swapan Sadhan (Tutu) Bose and Kanwar Deep Singh, nominated to the Rajya Sabha from West Bengal and Jharkhand, respectively, by the All-India Trinamool Congress (AITC) may be the only exceptions.

In matters of governance, however, the concern is for any mistake that she may make with no one having the guts to point it out to her. Mamata is aware of this image of hers and occasionally tries to correct her course but she can hardly help her tendency to be undiplomatic and tactless, whether she is talking about the judiciary or to anyone who has dared to question her in public: a farmer or a young student. Yet, she is known to have publicly accepted her mistakes. People have given her a massive mandate, fully aware of her 'negatives' because the main agenda for people across the board was to rid themselves of the Left. Everything else took a backseat. Even stability was not an issue.

Mamata Banerjee's occasional pitch against the Congress and Manmohan Singh is not exactly without reason. She is hoping for the emergence of a third front that will have a major say in the days to come. 'Either there is the Congress or there is the BJP. Why? Because there is no alternative. If there is such an option, people will think about it,' Mamata said in a television interview. The Trinamool's foray into four of the five poll-bound states was to test the waters on the party's acceptability beyond Bengal and to garner as many votes as possible to secure recognition as a national political party with the Central Election Commission. Mamata, however, is not expecting much at the moment. 'It may not happen in the first attempt but at least we have begun it... If there is a good leadership, Trinamool can make its presence felt in other states too,' she said.

Her poll managers have started drumming up support for Mamata as the 'viable alternative'. Says Sultan Ahmed, union minister of state for tourism and Trinamool's man in charge of Uttar Pradesh and Uttarakhand, 'We are telling people about her clean and pro-people image. People are tired of mainstream political parties.' Like-minded parties have already started sounding out the Trinamool. Mamata herself says, 'They believe we can provide justice to people.' In the elections held in five states in March 2012, the Trinamool Congress emerged as the second largest party in Manipur, winning seven seats in a house of 60 seats.

In her proximate circles, Mamata is known to have taken the centre's 'reluctance' to offer Bengal a bailout package as an affront to her. In an interview, she gave enough indications of this. 'For over two years, Trinamool does not even have an office there (in Parliament). We have only one cabinet minister—the ministers of state are not even allowed to work. We still keep quiet. Only on anti-people policies, we have refused to extend our support. Take the case of the Food Bill...where will the money come from? Unlike others, we do not say something at closed door meetings with the prime minister and something else outside,' she said. 'The Congress is a minority government. The government is there only because we are supporting it,' she reminded viewers.

Inspite of the Trinamool's simmering discontent, Mamata has never suggested that she would walk out of UPA-2, giving an opportunity to other parties to make up for her numbers. According to Trinamool insiders, she has indicated to her party leaders that if the Congress becomes weaker after the 2014 polls, the only alternative before her would be a strong bloc of like-minded parties to fill the void. Her plan is similar to that of the Left Front. She wants to consolidate her party's support base in rural Bengal in the upcoming panchayat elections and break borders to expand her party's influence in states like Manipur. She does not mind tying up with non-UPA regional parties, as long as it helps her cause.

Though equations may not remain the same when the country gets set for the Lok Sabha elections in 2014, the Trinamool does not foresee reverses in the party's prospects in Bengal. Party leaders feel that Mamata has been in government too short a time—only a year—to compare her to the Left Front with its thirty-four years of rule. Even if there is dissent in local pockets, it is not likely to change the voting pattern in Bengal in 2014. Partha Chatterjee believes that in the next Lok Sabha polls, the party will be able to send at least thirty-six members to Parliament which, taken together with its strength elsewhere, will help Mamata emerge as a crucial player in national politics.

The dilemma faced by Mamata is that she owes her success to the overwhelming support of the peasantry in rural areas, who realized that the 'industrialization and urbanization at any cost' policy of the CPI(M)-led government would lead to eviction of the peasantry on a huge scale. She secured middle class support courtesy the way the CPI(M) was capturing one organization after another, packing educational institutions with its yes-men and ruining the education and health infrastructure of the state. The middle class, however, wants industrialization and urbanization.

The media too, both print and electronic, is pushing hard for 'reforms', which means liberalization, privatization and urbanization. This would require the acquisition of land on a large scale. If she pursues the latter course, she loses the rural vote; if she sticks to her 'no acquisition of land by government' policy, she loses the middle class and media support. Will she be able to strike the right balance between the two contradictory pressures? Which side will she lean towards? On the answer to these questions depends, to a large extent, the future of the Trinamool Congress government in the state. The *aam aadmi* (*manush*) has invested his hope in Mamata Banerjee; it is in her that the poor in Bengal, especially in rural areas, increasingly see their salvation. Yet, the euphoria over the Left Front ouster will be short lived. The scanners will be out: Mamata's every move will be watched and voted upon. That will be her ultimate test.

Mamata in Power

> The great men and women of history are remembered
> not because they never made mistakes or never failed,
> but because they did not let their failures stop them.
> They kept on until they succeeded.
>
> —Gordon Parks

'I am satisfied. I may not be wrong in saying that we have completed 99 per cent of what we had set out to achieve.' Mamata Banerjee's self-assessment does not, however, ring true to the many ears that were expecting first-class governance. The first year in power has, of course, not been a holiday for the first-time chief minister. Re-engineering a system that has been roughly ridden; where decay has been nurtured and apathy cherished; where might has been right and the Left has always been right for thirty-four long years could have been nothing but a nightmare. One that has been lightened somewhat by the tremendous goodwill that the leader continues to enjoy despite the many disappointments, the fading euphoria and the reality of having to deal with empty coffers, sceptical industrialists, recalcitrant ultras, an intractable opposition, a bureaucracy reduced to impotence, and absent socio-economic infrastructure.

Converting a negative vote for the erstwhile incumbent to positive support driven by good governance is like asking for the moon under this complex web of circumstances. Yet the moon is what the chief minister had promised her people; it is still what she wants to give them. However, '*poriborton*' is proving to be a difficult mistress, when the agents of change—the administration, right from the top to the grassroots— have gotten used to a different way of doing things. Often even the state-level leadership is rendered totally helpless in rooting out the corrupt and undisciplined elements from the administration. They became a law unto themselves and acquiescence was the only option for the masses.

In her maiden press conference following her first cabinet meeting, Mamata Banerjee prioritized her job list: 'We have come to power on the mandate of the *gonodebota* and so we are dedicating our victory to the people of the state. The first resolution of our first cabinet meeting was to keep promises that we had made to the people and that was to return the 400 acres of land to those farmers of Singur who had been unwilling to let their land go in acquisitions made by the previous government.'

Mamata Banerjee's welcome assurance, as far as law and order were concerned, was: 'We will ensure that the police will work to protect democracy and rise above "partycracy".' At that time she meant it. The government, she said, would give the police a free hand to take action against all miscreants without caring for which political party they might belong to. In her first few days she made all the correct statements and right moves, reflecting a keenness for '*poriborton*' and making her style of governance all-inclusive. Possibly, her first press conference was free from any threat or rancour after her massive victory. She even invited the Tatas to set up their car plant in the remaining 600 acres of land.

What could also hardly have escaped notice is the manner in which her cadres kept their heads down and ensured that the victory celebrations were dignified and controlled. There was none of the inevitable post-election blood bath. This demonstrated both her political maturity and total control over her followers, which even young Akhilesh Yadav could not achieve recently in Uttar Pradesh, despite the guidance of the experienced Mulayam Singh Yadav.

To her credit, her government, acting on their poll promise, immediately initiated the necessary legislative and legal steps to facilitate the return of 400 acres of land to farmers in Singur. Predictably, this was challenged by Tata Motors and, following the single bench ruling in the government's favour, the division bench of Calcutta High Court reversed the decision in favour of Tata Motors. The government's appeal lies with the Supreme Court of India. Meanwhile, the people of Bengal—those who lost land in Singur and elsewhere, in particular—are getting impatient.

The Left is, of course, back to fishing in troubled waters. Rumours are rife that Singur will switch its loyalty back to the Left, something that the Singur Trinamool MLA Becharam Manna strongly refutes. The 2013 panchayat polls is, therefore, crucial for Mamata Banerjee. Her decision to give additional responsibility of the panchayat department to the powerful veteran, Subrata Mukherjee, is an indication of the importance she attaches to the panchayat polls, which will be a precursor to the Lok Sabha polls in 2014. In the recently announced results, TMC, as expected, has swept the polls beyond its own expectations.

Jangalmahal is the other tricky business. Mamata has promised that government will, on one hand, conduct a dialogue as soon as possible and on the other hand, initiate development activities. To be fair to her, the humanitarian approach and healing touch has made a difference in the hills, especially in Darjeeling, and as well as in Jangalmahal. As union minister Jairam Ramesh commented recently, 'Mamata's holding and kissing a tribal child is much more effective in Jangalmahal than any police operation.' In her foreword to the publication *Promises Delivered*, brought out by the state information and cultural affairs department on her completing one year in office, Mamata writes, 'People of both the hills and Jangalmahal are all smiles.' Not everyone is smiling, though; certainly not those who have experienced her high-handedness in addressing sensitive issues.

There are several such instances. The recent arrest of Shiladitya Chowdhury, branded as Maoist, at the behest of Mamata Banerjee, for daring to question the chief minister on fertilizer prices at her rally in West Midnapur's Belpahari on 8 August 2012 is one. Another is the cartoon controversy when a Jadavpur University professor was arrested a few months ago for poking fun at the chief minister.

Press Council of India chairman Markanday Katju protested, saying, 'Her action is most undemocratic, to say the least. I had earlier given a statement in favour of Mamata Banerjee because I thought one should see good points in a person's personality also. But now I have changed my opinion and believe that she is totally undeserving to be a political leader in a democratic country like India since she has no respect for the Constitutional and civil rights of citizens and is totally dictatorial, intolerant and whimsical in her behaviour.' Political rivals lost no opportunity to strike out at the Trinamool with the CPI(M) alleging that the arrest amounted to autocracy and slammed Mamata for not being ready to listen to any criticism or question. Even Magsaysay awardee Mahashweta Devi said, 'That he spoke frankly...is his fault? This should have been avoided.'

Nevertheless, Mamata's initiatives in Jangalmahal are bearing fruit. The government's emphasis on the uplift and development of socio-economic conditions of the people of Jangalmahal under the newly-created Paschimanchal Unnayan Affairs Department are steps in the right direction. Her unequivocal condemnation of violence has also made a difference, with some 22 Maoist activists surrendering before her. Incidents of violence have dropped considerably: only 32 in July-December 2011, down from 2003 the year before.

The Gorkhaland issue is also being resolved. It was to the credit of the Mamata government that, within months of coming to power, a memorandum of agreement was signed between the government of India, the government of West Bengal and the Gorkha Janmukti Morcha (GJM) on 18 July 2011. The Gorkhaland Territorial Administration (GTA) Bill 2011 has been passed by the West Bengal Legislative Assembly and is awaiting the assent of the President.

The biggest '*poriborton*' in West Bengal, obviously, involves Mamata Banerjee's transformation from opposition leader to chief minister. Many of the jarring notes emanating from her are a product of the mental clash between these two roles. Where Mamata Banerjee has carried the day is with her initial sound bytes that were pragmatic and positive; save for her comments on her ally, the state Congress, the centre and with regard to some segments of industry. Her suggestion, 'let industry find its own land', smacks of a leader who is not ready to embrace industry and is probably a throwback to the Singur crisis.

Land in West Bengal is one of the key ingredients for development of industries as well as infrastructure. When Pavan Poddar, a leading industrialist and president of a business chamber, said in the presence of the state's commerce and industries minister Partha Chatterjee that procurement and delivery of land had become a very sensitive issue and that a practical, pragmatic and transparent policy for making available land for industrial as well as infrastructural development was the need of the hour, the minister engaged in some tight-rope walking. He admitted that land resources in West

Bengal were limited but assured him that land acquisition would not be an issue. He said that the government would scrutinize the reason for the acquisition as well as the significance and the impact of the specific acquisition.

At other places, there has clearly been mismanagement. The issue of the Nonadanga evictions has flared up, with the Left seizing the opportunity to accuse Mamata of deserting her pro-poor and anti-eviction policy after coming to power. Rebel Trinamool MP Kabir Suman lost no time in penning a song—'*Singur theke Nonadanga*' ('From Singur to Nonadanga')—depicting the party's changing face, from one that fought against eviction of small farmers in Singur to one that was evicting the Nonadanga settlers without offering any rehabilitation. Kabir Suman says, 'The way the police attacked a peaceful rally, the way the police minister (Mamata Banerjee) stopped a peaceful demonstration and arrested the agitators, makes me realize that the *Ma-Mati-Manush* is under siege.' Mamata has realized that it is a Catch 22 situation and is trying to proceed with caution. Yet there are clear signs of a shift in Trinamool policy. The mindset of governance is slowly getting the better of the opposition.

Development projects held up under the earlier regime because of Trinamool opposition are also coming back to haunt her now. There is the proposed revival by the TMC government of the 4.5 km long Kukrahati-Raichak Bridge that the Left Front had planned in 2006. It had to be abandoned in the face of the Trinamool Congress's agitation against land acquisition. Roads are a must and Bengal's finance minister Amit Mitra is busy projecting the industry-friendly image of the state, trying to counter the damage caused by inadvertent statements and negative perceptions. At a meeting with Kolkata's leading business chambers, he said, 'We are a business-friendly government. Our government wants growth along with employment generation. It is business that creates employment. We want a seamless relationship with industry.' Such seamlessness demands a relationship that Mamata Banerjee will have to walk miles to achieve. Meanwhile, there are other positions, emotions and sentiments that have to be balanced.

The fact of the matter is that Mamata Banerjee is basically a socialist and, therefore, not really anti-Left, though she is opposed to the 'present band of Communists', to quote a close associate. According to him, she dislikes and distrusts capitalists and does not feel comfortable in their company. It almost sounded similar to what was being said about Buddhadeb Bhattacharya till he became industry's blue-eyed chief minister. Mamata's vote bank is the state's poor and it is important for her to preserve her pro-poor image even if it means keeping industry and, more importantly, Kolkata's business community at arm's length.

In her one-year term as chief minister, Mamata Banerjee has not accepted a single invitation from any business chamber in the city. That assignment she has left to the industry minister, Partha Chatterjee. Nor does she welcome photo-ops with businessmen, denying entry to press photographers to the couple of informal interactive meetings that she has held with industrialists. She apprehends that some businessmen may misuse these photographs with her. Businessmen in Kolkata—or, for that matter, anywhere—are known for displaying blown-up photographs with dignitaries in their offices.

The mistrust is mutual, though, and there lies the rub. Kolkata-based industrialists are yet to reconcile to the fact of Mamata being the chief minister of West Bengal. Financial support to her party has been more out of compulsion than love for the TMC or its leader. Strange though it may sound, my interaction with the business community leaves me in no doubt that it still hopes and prays for the return of the Left Front. Indeed, it is a strange situation with capitalists rooting for Communists, leading to doubts about the ideological credentials of the Communists!

As the president of a business chamber said, 'They are neither Communists nor Marxists but behave like good Congressmen.' Significantly, JSW Ispat Steel Ltd, which is putting up a much talked about steel plant at Salboni, is in the process of shifting its registered office from Kolkata to Mumbai. A notice dated 2 May 2012 has been circulated, seeking shareholder approval. Big business houses are not only waiting and watching but also shifting. Obviously, their confidence level is low given the lack of direct and comfortable rapport with the chief minister.

Whatever be the final outcome of this duel between government and industry, the government is, for the first time, asking questions, the answers to which should have been with the government to begin with. Thus, even while wanting to build relations with industry, the government demanded a transparency that the state had forgotten to look for. Not only has the TMC government asked business chambers for a list of unused land given to their members, it has also asked its joint venture partners, particularly those in the housing sector, for details of profit sharing in the form of payment of dividends against the shares held by the government. These are perfectly legitimate enquiries, but in the cozy club of government and industry fostered by the earlier regime, such questions do send worrying ripples down the spines of those business partners who have been less than fair to the government.

Then came the shocking fire at Amri Hospital that took a savage toll of patients' lives and ended in the arrest of many of the businessmen directors on the Amri Hospital board. The directors were refused bail for a very long time, exacerbating the sense of mistrust. In an unprecedented move, business chambers made it an issue between the government and industry and issued strong press statements that, obviously, did not amuse the TMC supremo. Even the Pradesh Congress Committee slammed the TMC government over the Amri arrests. The PCC spokesman Abdul Mannan said, 'We are cautioning the government. These arrests are sending a wrong message to the people. While the guilty ones need to be punished, innocent people must not be harassed.'

Meanwhile, the continued denial of bail to the Amri accused by the Court was interpreted by some as a parochial, Bengali versus Marwari issue. The chief minister was furious and saw in it a game plan by vested interests to destabilize her government. However, showing great restraint and maturity, she said in an interview to Hindi daily *Sanmarg*, 'Marwaris are as Bengali as I am'; a statement well appreciated by the community. In a letter, the representative body of the Marwari community, the All-India Marwari Sammelan, welcomed the statement: 'Your statement reflects the sentiments and feelings of all sections of the people irrespective of their caste, creed, language, origin or religion. Your statement has been welcomed by one and all and will go a long way in allaying any apprehension and misunderstanding. Your statement conveys an assurance, if it was needed, that justice will be non-discriminating and fair. Any scope of apprehension on this score is totally misplaced.'

The letter was sent to the chief minister's office and residence but there was no acknowledgement, according to the office bearers of the organization. A few days later, a senior minister of her cabinet complained to a leading businessman that, 'the CM is not happy that your community did not even welcome such a positive statement.' Clearly, there is a feedback problem within the government. According to the organization, a copy of the statement was handed over to the businessman with a request to forward it to the minister concerned to bring it to the notice of the chief minister.

There have been other instances of strategic symbolism. Mamata Banerjee's visit to Birla Park to greet the patriarch Basant Kumar Birla and his wife Sarala Birla on their 70th wedding anniversary did a great deal to assuage the hurt feelings of the Marwari community. It is understood that painter Shuvaprasanna, known to be close to her, convinced the chief minister with the logic that 'the marriage had been supervised by none other than Mahatma Gandhi.' Mamata said, 'I have listened to my heart and have come here.' The industry minister Partha Chatterjee was prompt to draw a connection: 'The visit showed the government's keenness on industrialization. The message is clear.' Such symbolism is welcome but needs to be translated into serious policy enactments, which are still to come.

Normally the first year of any new government is considered to be a 'honeymoon' period; when the opposition is demoralized and refrains from criticizing strongly because of its own loss of credibility. For Mamata Banerjee, despite a still demoralized opposition and some notable successes, the first year has been far from a bed of roses with the new government dealing with too many thorny issues. Some became more irksome because the newly elected government was not trained in the art of governance at a time that the voters were expecting 'Ram Rajya'; in the genuine hope that the TMC in power could dispel the agony of years of dispossession like magic.

Large sections, particularly in rural and semi-urban Bengal, still look to Mamata for a *Sonar Bangla*. They have lost neither hope nor belief in Mamata. Meanwhile, the chief minister herself is learning the art of pragmatism; erring now and again; occasionally losing her equanimity in public and appearing to be arrogant. Sometimes, she does not seem to practice what she preaches. 'Work more, talk less' is what she believes in but it can be said without fear of contradiction that Mamata is India's most talkative chief minister. She loves to talk; she briefs the press herself everyday; often more than once a day. Her emotions brim over, sometimes with unfortunate results for herself and those who serve her state.

Within days of her taking over, on 26 May 2011, on her way to the Writers' Building, Mamata Banerjee stopped her car in front of the Bangur Institute of Neurosciences on Sambhunath Pandit Road in Kolkata for a surprise visit. Upset with what seemed to her to be a non-cooperative attitude, she suspended Shyamapada Ghorai from the post of director of the hospital on the spot. The doctor was charged with 'misconduct by non-cooperation with the chief minister during her surprise visit'. Ghorai, considered to be a hard-working doctor doing his best in trying circumstances, remains suspended at the time of the writing but there has been no visible improvement in the state-run hospital.

The *bhadralok* intellectuals of West Bengal, for long aloof—almost portraying Mamata as an untouchable—suddenly started warming up to the chief minister in the last phase of her successful campaign to oust the Left. Indeed, the so-called literati, considered to be sympathetic to the Left, became the champions of change. For Mamata Banerjee, who looked at these 'cultural czars' not only with suspicion but also contempt, they were a God-sent gift on the eve of elections that she embraced with warmth. Image-building was vital for her to garner support from the middle-class and this she managed, though never eschewing her primary constituency: the under classes, slum dwellers and street-fighters, whom Ashok Mitra calls the 'lumpens'. To be honest, Mamata has greater faith in these lumpens who, she knows, will not desert her; she has no such faith in the literati and urban middle class.

Mamata Banerjee is right, in a way. The first to question the unquestionable Mamata was a leading member of the literati: the well-known musician and activist Kabir Suman, a Trinamool

Congress MP from the Jadavpur constituency in Kolkata. 'Mamata's various paranoid acts read like a script. And all for domination. The same authoritarianism against which we were fighting. But that was different Mamata,' says a fiercely independent Suman in a signed article in *Outlook* (30 April 2012), almost on the eve of first anniversary of the Trinamool government. 'However, it is not that I want her to vacate the chief minister's post but she should mend her ways.' His response to the arrest of Ambikesh Mahapatra in the 'Cartoongate' incident was a song mocking the Mamata Banerjee government, titled: '*Hashi Niye Thako*' (Keep Smiling). Suman asks the people of Bengal to smile even in pain: '*Hashi Niye Thako/ Hashi mukhe thako/Bongo rongo hok; sob lok heshe nik jantranateo*'.

It all started with the post-midnight arrest of fifty-two-year old Ambikesh Mahapatra, professor of Jadavpur University and seventy-two-year old retired engineer, Subrata Sengupta, for allegedly forwarding a Mamata Banerjee cartoon, which was doing the rounds on the Internet. The accused were charged with trying to outrage her modesty; the professor was beaten up outside the gate of his co-operative housing society in Kolkata, allegedly by local TMC workers. The incident jolted the people of West Bengal. The *Telegraph* put the story on the front page under the headline: 'Sonar Bangle (golden bangle): If you are still not wearing such handcuffs in Bengal, *Subha Naboborsho* (Happy New Year)'.

The arrest took place on 13 April 2012 on the eve of the Bengali New Year. Even a vocal Mamata supporter, eminent economist Abhirup Sarkar, reacted with horror. 'This is very autocratic. This scares me.' Sukanta Chaudhuri, professor emeritus at Jadavpur University, said, 'If any criticism of the government becomes an insult to women, any speech becomes impossible.' Although the three lines in the cartoon were loosely based on dialogues in Satyajit Ray's 1974 film *Sonar Kella* (Golden Fortress), where the magician makes the 'naughty man' disappear to please the child Mukul.

The political message was clear—the golden fortress (the railways portfolio) had been taken away from 'unreliable' Dinesh Trivedi and given by Mamata to her 'own man', Mukul Roy.

What intrigued people more on the national level was the other character in the cartoon who had been dealt with by Mamata Banerjee: her own senior party colleague, to whom she had given the railways portfolio. Admittedly, Mukul Roy was her first choice for the position but he was not acceptable to the prime minister, who insisted on the more suave and savvy Dinesh Trivedi. The fracas over the railway budget too had more to do with intra-party discipline than the railway finances or the travails of the ordinary Indian.

It an unprecedented move, the railway budget was opposed by the party that was represented by the railway minister! By all accounts, Dinesh Trivedi presented a forward-looking budget that ran counter to Mamata Banerjee's diktat and was immediately put on notice by the party chief. Dinesh took the high moral ground, saying, 'I cannot let people die in accidents. For me country comes first and then the family, followed by the party.' Mamata, who controls her party with an iron grip saw this as a bigger game in which Trivedi was being encouraged to go against her party line by the Congress, to weaken her.

The backdrop to this story is interesting. US-educated, Gujarati Dinesh Trivedi, also a trained pilot, was introduced to Mamata Banerjee by former Prime Minister V.P. Singh. Dinesh was with the Singh-led Janata Dal till 1998 and Mamata needed someone who could lobby for her, not only in the corridors of power in Delhi but also with big business houses. Dinesh fitted the bill. Ironically, the Dinesh Trivedi cameo compares with that of his political mentor V.P. Singh, who was patronized by Indira Gandhi and Rajiv Gandhi but, on being appointed as defence minister, started probing defence deals, including the infamous Bofors deal involving Rajiv Gandhi himself. He was dismissed from the cabinet, quit the party and the rest is history. The question is, will history repeat itself?

Whatever the history, two features revealed themselves during the drama over the railway budget: the helplessness of the UPA-2 government in the face of coalition compulsions and the Congress' machinations to 'break the TMC game', given the clear disenchantment of some eminent members of the Mamata flock. Of her 19 MPs, two—Kabir Suman and Dinesh Trivedi—have been in open rebellion. If rumours in Delhi are to be believed, 10 other TMC parliamentarians are 'angry and aggrieved' and are being egged on by the Congress to defect. This is now an open secret. Trinamool MP and former West Bengal Pradesh Congress Committee president Somen Mitra does not deny this and says, 'Yes, I was approached by the Congress, but of course I declined.'

Somen Mitra, once a Congress strongman in Bengal, is still considered powerful. Trinamool MLA Madan Mitra did not mince words, calling it the 'Congress's vain attempt to break us up.' He told the press, 'It is a case of a dying party trying to prey on a party that is alive,' thus confirming the rumours. Madan Mitra, who has been recently elevated to cabinet rank as minister for transport and sports, is considered to be close to Mamata.

The WBPCC general secretary, Om Prakash Mishra, made the most striking observation.'Yes, it is happening but it is the other way round. The approach is being made by the disgruntled TMC leaders,' he chuckles. 'We will make the most of it, if there is defection to our side as per law.' Rumours are that about a dozen out of 19 Lok Sabha MPs and 70 MLAs out of the TMC's 184 are disgruntled. However, with the Congress government itself being in the doldrums at the centre, any major bid to upset the applecart seems doubtful; at least for the time being. Some reports are making headlines and not all are off-the-record statements.

Mamata Banerjee is perfectly aware of these developments. The dismissal of Trivedi as railway minister served the dual purpose of stoutly opposing a fare hike and sending a message to her core constituency of the poor and underprivileged, and nipping in the bud any possible revolt within the party. It also sent a stern message to the Congress that it should not play around with the TMC. The Congress too has realized that while it would be happy to dump Mamata, given the political circumstances, it would be more prudent to have her on their side. The more relevant point is that Bengal does not offer the political space for two anti-Left parties.

The other point of note is that historically, the Congress has suffered most whenever it has aligned with local regional parties. Starting with Tamil Nadu, the Congress has lost its position as principal opposition party in states from Uttar Pradesh to Bihar. The present Congress-TMC alliance is already under strain. Om Prakash Mishra's interview to *Frontline* (5-18 May 2012) is strikingly frank. 'We do not want a break but we do not mind a break-up,' he said. Meanwhile, both the Congress and the CPI(M) are using the same language, even the same phraseology, to run the TMC down.

Reacting to the state government publication *Promises Delivered* on the first anniversary of the TMC government, the leader of the opposition, Surya Kanta Mishra, called it a 'government of announcements'. Asked to respond to the chief minister's claim of having achieved 99 per cent of the work she had set out to do, Om Prakash Mishra says, 'It is a government of announcements and pronouncements. The chief minister is in a self-congratulating mode all the time.' The Congress spokesman was speaking more like the opposition than an alliance partner. 'The TMC speaks the language of ultimatums, deadlines and now, even the social boycott of the opposition. It attempts to muzzle the press and restrict the freedom of expression.' These words, coming from TMC's partner in the government and that, too, within less than a year of coming to power, must be like music to the ears of the CPI(M) leaders.

Mamata Banerjee seems to be satisfied with her performance, though. In one of her rare interviews to the Kolkata edition of a national English daily she said, while evaluating her year's rule, that she had accomplished '99 per cent of what we had set out to achieve.' She highlights her manifold achievements, in addition to success in Darjeeling and Jangalmahal. 'There is Rs 85,000 crore worth of investment in the pipeline. There are new opportunities too. A total of 5,00,000 people have gained employment. Land ceiling laws have been relaxed.' The prompt Left rejoinder from the leader of the opposition, Surya Kant Mishra, '*Jobab Meleni*' (Questions Unanswered), did not score too many points, though. It did not really fault any basic TMC policy.

In fact, it supports the demand of three years' moratorium on payment of interest on total debt. While ridiculing the chief minister's claim of 99 per cent of targets achieved, Surya Kanta Mishra admits, 'A year is too short a period to evaluate a government.' A party in power for thirty-four years should know that. What '*Jobab Meleni*' refers to are recent incidents of rape with a 'political vengeance', assault on teachers, murders of rival political party leaders, partisan action or total inaction of police, farmers' suicides and such others. The hullabaloo over some of them is the result of immature and off-the-cuff, stray statements either by the chief minister herself or by her ministerial colleagues. Food minister Jyotipriya Mullick's advisory to TMC functionaries not to marry into families with CPI(M) links is one such example which left the TMC a bit red in the face. The silence amongst civil society on this issue was quite deafening.

Trinamool insiders confirm that Mamata is concerned over the increasing alienation of the urban middle class, including a section of intellectuals who, not very long ago, were her vocal supporters. The party's image has suffered recently in the wake of frequent controversies caused by inept handling of situations by a section of Trinamool leaders. These range from the call of a minister to socially boycott the Communists to direct interference at the local police station level. The infighting between trade union leaders has led to a multiplicity of TMC unions, creating unrest on the industrial front. Reportedly, instructions have been issued to ministers to refrain from making rash statements. Former Bhangor MLA Arabul Islam has finally been asked to surrender before a court and there is the need to instill some discipline. He had been absconding and police had been unable to arrest him, since they were under government pressure. To avoid continued bad publicity he was asked to surrender. Mamata Banerjee is quite capable of disciplining the party but the need sometimes is to discipline the chief minister herself.

The position of chief minister is invested with a sense of responsibility that members of the opposition and its leaders can often escape. Mamata Banerjee needs to check herself from making 'rash' remarks and creating unpleasant situations. Within days of her meeting with her core party leaders to formulate a strategy to save the party from such goof-ups, a fuming Mamata walked out of a national television show after calling young students 'CPM cadres and Maoists', in what was a public relations disaster for the TMC and its leader.

Ironically, the interactive session 'Question Time Didi' was organized by television channel CNN-IBN to mark the first anniversary of TMC rule in West Bengal, and would have provided a great opportunity to present to the nation the good work done by her government. Her inability to take questions from students in the spirit in which they were asked clearly exposed the paranoid state of the chief minister's mind. Indeed, Mamata Banerjee could have used the opportunity to win over students—had they actually been from the opposition camp—but she decided that anyone, even college girls, were the enemy because they asked difficult questions. Indeed, she proved her tendency to be her own worst enemy even as she is the biggest strength of the Trinamool Congress.

Mamata Banerjee is nothing if not unpredictable. She does not believe anybody and sees an enemy in everybody. Her obsession with her lower-middle class background is sometimes a handicap. Indeed, her background has often been the butt of opposition campaigns that have brought up her background, upbringing, education, alleged fake degree and so much more that one senses a feeling of paranoia when she is confronted with her background. Yet the opposition attacking her family background only meant that they did not have much else to attack her with—something that Mamata Banerjee could have used to good effect. She could also have ignored it but she allowed herself to be affected by it to the extent that even those close to her suspect that she suffers from an inferiority complex because of her background.

One does not have to be a psychiatrist to know that one suffering from a sense of inferiority often tries to go overboard to establish or demonstrate one's superiority; even when it is totally unnecessary. It is clear that Mamata Banerjee may be falling prey to her own internal dilemmas. There have been outstanding leaders at the state and national level who came from humble backgrounds, who were not educated in English—Lal Bahadur Shastri and Atal Bihari Vajpayee, to name two. They rose to become highly respected prime ministers of India. Mamata Banerjee never misses a chance to talk about her humble background but somehow conveys the sense that she holds it responsible for her inability to secure universal acceptance as a leader, without realizing that it is her personal idiosyncrasies that make people look at her askance, not her pedigree.

It is curious that she should feel thus, given the massive mandate that she received with almost the whole of Bengal's intelligentsia standing by her as she took on the formidable Left. She has, over the years, emerged as a competent orator and a consummate though quirky politician. These quirks do neither her nor her party any good. As far as her colleagues in the party are concerned, from commanding respect, Mamata now commands fear. While this fear factor is to some extent needed in today's cruel and cut-throat politics with ever-wavering loyalty, beyond a point it becomes counter-productive.

Indeed, Mamata has a cabinet but no colleagues; there is no team in a need-based relationship that she has instituted. The need changes with the time and situation; so do relationships, where one of the parties has no voice. Mamata does not believe in giving even her senior colleagues a voice or providing space for them to make suggestions. She knows that the buck stops with her and would not have it any other way. However, while all this may make her a complex personality, it does not diminish the monumental feat that she has achieved.

No one else would have dared to take on the Left Front, or braved such hostility in unwavering pursuit of her goal. In a world which has seen the virtual decimation of the Communists, Bengal, within democratic India, seemed to be the last fortress of the Left and once Mamata breached it, her profile soared high both nationally and internationally. She figures among *Time* magazine's top 100 influential people in the world. The Left may be dismissive—the leader of the opposition Surya Kant Mishra said, 'If they (*Time* magazine) had asked for my permission to put my name in it, I would have refused'—but Mamata did not lobby for such recognition. She won it on the basis of her remarkable achievement.

India Today's 16 April 2012 issue profiling the 50 powerful people of India placed Mamata Banerjee in the fourth position, only after Sonia Gandhi, Pranab Mukherjee and Manmohan Singh. This was recognition for almost single-handedly defeating the Left Front in West Bengal after thirty-four years of uninterrupted rule; for not allowing power to corrupt her financially; for being the only rebel Congress women to have reduced the erstwhile party to a minor party in her state; for being the only voice in her one-woman party; and, most importantly, for her party being the single largest coalition partner of the UPA-2 government at the centre, thereby influencing most of India's political, economic, social and even foreign policy decisions.

Yet, it is not India that Mamata currently wants to run; it is her own state that she wants to serve. Her moves to defend the federal structure of government have given birth to a new political force in India, with several chief ministers—Nitish Kumar of Bihar, Naveen Patnaik of Odisha, J. Jayalalitha of Tamil Nadu, Narendra Modi of Gujarat and several others—coming on the same page. Where she errs is in not tempering her impulsiveness with the tact that she is capable of using. Much more could have been achieved with quiet diplomacy than with public and vocal confrontation with the centre. That might be good for the galleries or even her fragile ego but not for the economic and political advantage of West Bengal, which is her eventual objective.

The moot question today is about how the mandate can be converted into socio-economic gains for the long neglected state. At a recent meeting, the German Consul-General in Kolkata publicly stated that with the Communists out of power, the climate for investment should improve. India's 'Look East' policy is dependent largely on the states in eastern India, particularly West Bengal, whose border with several neighbouring countries has strategic importance. Away from all the political rhetoric, what the state needs is strategic moves to secure the opportunities knocking on the door. No such strategy is yet obvious even though a great many things are being attempted simultaneously.

The success and survival of Mamata Banerjee will depend on her ability to win friends and influence people. It will equally depend on professional management and sound governance. There are changes waiting to happen in West Bengal: agricultural, academic, economic, infrastructural and cultural. Not everything depends on the centre or on land; not everything can be explained away by competently prepared excuses. Governance is about addressing problems; not wishing them away. It is about fixing problems, not assigning blame; finding solutions not excuses. Not everything depends on political machinations or heading a third front at the centre. A lot of useful work is to be done in the state; work that demands intelligence, integrity and an insistent search for results. Politics is, in the end, the art of achieving the impossible.

Epilogue

The result of the West Bengal panchayat elections, announced on July 30-31, 2013 is proving to be Mamata Banerjee's *Long March* and a flashback on her spectacular assembly election triumph a little over two years ago. The only exception is that this time round the Trinamool Congress has trounced both the CPI(M) and the Congress in three-cornered elections. The TMC's undisputed dominance over rural Bengal remains almost intact as she bettered the 2008 verdict by capturing thirteen of the seventeen zilla parishad boards and seized control of a majority of the 341 panchayat samitis. The small setback in semi-urban pockets bordering Kolkata only serves to remind one of the fact that the Left too dominated rural Bengal for over three decades with similar hesitant support from Kolkata and semi-urban areas. History is repeating itself, it seems.

In my first chapter I had summed up the change in the following words: 'It may well turn out to be a turning point in the post-Independence political history of the state and the country. It may also turn out to be a damp squib unless the new rulers quickly master the art of governance. The bottom line is that Bengal is unique and good governance in Bengal must be uniquely suited to this state.'

There was hope with the slogan Ma, Mati, Manush, which indicated a commitment to women, to land and the people. Without all three progress could hardly be all inclusive and in all spheres in the state. What then is the balance sheet after little more than two years? Where does Chief Minister Mamata Banerjee stand today? Much water has flown down the river Ganges under the Howrah Bridge since I wrote this book's last two chapters, coincidentally titled 'Ma, Mati, Manush' and 'Mamata in Power'.

First, consider the claims of the government. One positive achievement undoubtedly has been that the clashes with the Maoists in the Jangalmahal area have almost disappeared with the retreat, at least for the time being, of the Maoists to their hideouts. Another has been the relative calm, again for the time being, prevailing in the Darjeeling area even though the Gorkha Janmukti Morcha (GMM) has revved up the movement with the announcement of the bifurcation of Andhra Pradesh to create a separate 29th state of the Indian Union, Telangana. The Gorkhaland demand has sprung back to life in Bengal. Bimal Gurung stepped down as Chief Administrator, Gorkha Territorial Administration (GTA), announcing a renewed movement. Mamata's formula of greater autonomy through the GTA to placate statehood sentiments in the hills and her tactful handling seems to be paying dividends.

On the economic front the record is far from pleasing. The demand of a large section of the people for industrialization has not been met, though there is some merit in the claim that small and medium industries have grown appreciably. The stumbling block for more rapid industrialization, particularly of large industries and big business enterprises, has been availability of land along with the insistence of the TMC government that industrialists must themselves negotiate with the peasants for land, which the government would not procure for private industry. Mamata Banerjee has publicly expressed her displeasure with the functioning of the industry ministry, holding it responsible for the state's failure to attract investment.

The industry department has been claiming that West Bengal has received investment proposals worth more than Rs 100,000 lakh crore since the change of guard. According to data in budget documents though, only twelve projects worth Rs 312.28 crore were implemented in 2011-12. However, business chamber leaders and businessmen do not hold the industry minister Partha Chatterjee responsible for poor response. They stress on the need for flexibility on the part of Chief Minister in her policies to accommodate the concerns of industry. Two major road projects in Bengal on the national highways, valued at Rs 800 crore are stuck over land issues.

Agriculture seems to be in a state of stagnation and even decline. Rice production in Bengal has dropped from 155 lakh tonnes in 2009-2010 to 140 lakh tonnes in 2012-13. If Bengal is hit by drought this year, the output will decline to around 130 lakh tonnes, casting a shadow on the rural economy because nearly 70 per cent of the population in Bengal depends on agriculture as the primary source of income. The bulk of Bengal's rice production, 110 lakh tonnes out of 150 lakh tonnes is dependent on monsoon rains as the state does not have the necessary irrigation network to facilitate rice cultivation in the boro (winter) season, when rainfall is negligible.

Admittedly, it is the Left Front's thirty-four year rule that should be blamed for the lack of irrigation facilities in Bengal, where only 15 lakh hectares of the 42 lakh hectares of cultivable area is covered by river-based irrigation. However, the TMC government, despite swearing by farmers, has not done much to improve things. No capital intensive major irrigation system has been taken up because there are no resources. Mamata Banerjee, who won election on Ma, Mati, Manush plank has been laying stress on *'Jal Dharo, Jal Bharo'* (collect water, fill water).

More worrying—and in popular perception the big failure of the TMC—is the government's inability to check the cycle of violence and counter violence that was a serious problem in the closing years of Left Front rule. Violence against women that is, of course, endemic in all parts of the country has increased in West Bengal and the government seems to be unable to control it. Kolkatans have been proud that their city has been the safest for women in India. Things have soured, especially in last one year. Living in fear of being molested in a city that welcomes Ma Durga every year but abuses ordinary women in a million ways every day is one of the many contradictions that needs to be corrected. It is as if all the psychos in Kolkata have suddenly been told there would be no consequences for their action: 'Do what you like, no one will stop you.'

The violators have become unafraid. Mamata's casual comments on the rising numbers of rape cases have not been well taken. She said, 'earlier, if men and women held hands, they would get caught by parents and reprimanded but now everything is so open. It is like an open market with open options.' During the election campaign she had earned kudos for her statement *bodol chai badla noy* (we want change not revenge). Yet, her cadres are doing precisely that: seeking revenge. Some of the statements from the Chief Minister herself seem to indicate an attempt to belittle the gravity of the situation.

Her supporters, of course, point to the Bantala episode in the Jyoti Basu regime when he tried to brush aside the incident that involved the rape and murder of two women. Having come to power on the slogan of change, however, Mamata Banerjee's attempt to seek shelter behind the argument that this was happening earlier shows the insensitivity of her government to an issue that has darkened the image of the country all over the world and is totally unacceptable in civilized society.

Violence is not new to Kolkata and West Bengal. All political parties have always had their own army of anti-socials surviving and thriving on the patronage of their political masters. It is also not new knowledge that the police, in its own interest, prefers to completely surrender to the political masters. Violence and lawlessness are interlinked with economic growth and the ambience for investment. Lack of employment and income-generating opportunities are made worse by the absence of new major investment, leading to a vicious cycle of hopelessness. Increasing violence is a reflection of this reality.

The rising incidents of sexual crimes against women, including assaults on foreign tourists, though not confined to only West Bengal, have prompted Mamata Banerjee to set up a separate anti-rape squad to make the city safer for women as it was proudly known to be. Bengal consistently ranking highest in crimes against women over the last two years is a matter of deep concern and shame.

The local TMC leaders are their own worst enemies, creating problems and earning bad publicity by their inexplicably offensive comments. 'If independent candidates give threats, damage and set fire to their houses, if the administration thinks of supporting the independents, you hurl bombs at the police and administration. I am telling you,' said Anubrata Mandal, the TMC Birbhum district president. Within days of his openly inciting his party supporters at the Kasba village, the father of independent candidate, Hriday Ghosh, was shot dead. Mamata Banerjee has publicly defended him though the West Bengal Human Rights Commission, taking cognizance of the case, has ordered the Birbhum SP to submit a report within a month.

One had hoped that the magnitude of her achievements in defeating a well entrenched government would lead to a sense of humility and bring about some maturity. Instead, one finds arrogance. One had also hoped that her transition from street fighter to Chief Minister would help her realize that she would need team work and have to delegate responsibility rather than attempt to do everything single handed. This has quite clearly led to discontent among the members of her cabinet, who are a demoralized lot without any zest to deal with the challenges that face the government from an opposition that is keen to regroup and begin its counter offensive.

Dinesh Trivedi, Minister of Parliament among the founders of the TMC, lost his Railway Ministry portfolio incurring the wrath of his leader for being too independent and is in the process of rehabilitating himself. Asked to comment on the functioning of the state government, he frankly admitted: 'For effective governance, cohesive functioning is required. I admit there are some problems. It is important to feel being part of a team. It is lacking.'

While it is true that the complete failure of the Congress leadership in West Bengal to challenge the Left Front over the years—permitting the Left front to win election after election—forced Mamata Banerjee to break away from the Congress and form her own party that became the focal point around which all anti-Left forces could unite, she had fought the 2011 election in alliance with the Congress even though she could probably have won on her own. It was the alliance that enabled her to achieve virtually a clean sweep. In a coalition, there are obviously differences of opinion or else there would not have been different parties. Dizzy with success, Mamata Banerjee was quick to jettison the alliance partner.

Notwithstanding the latest win, there is little doubt that the slide in her popularity has begun even if only in the urban areas. Mamata Banerjee has overestimated her own strength and is getting more and more isolated. She has ignored the lesson of history that when in power you need to broaden the alliance rather than restrict it by breaking with your own partners. There are clear indications that even within her own party she is getting isolated. She is feared by her cabinet colleagues rather than respected and loved.

Mamata's 'Ekla Chalo' (go it alone) thinking got a boost after the Jangipur by-poll, where the Congress's margin shrank by more than 1.2 lakh votes, even with the candidate being the son of President of India, Pranab Mukherjee, and the Left losing as many as 48,000 votes. Mamata directed her central ministers to resign and subsequently withdrew the support from UPA-2 on 18 September 2012. She was at her bitterest best on foreign direct investment, declaring that 'selling the country cannot be reforms. If you sell out, the people will boot you out—that is the beauty of democracy'. She followed it up by seeking to unseat the UPA-2 government democratically, by announcing her plan to sponsor a no-trust motion against the government.

She had overestimated her strength and failed to grasp the politics of north-Indian regional parties, which are governed by their self-interest than national interest. Power decides their policies. However, Mamata bolstered her credentials as protestor-in-chief against the reform measures in the process. Egged by support of various varieties of Yadav leaders, she even dreamt of a blueprint of a national government under her leadership. Her young advisors were not only immature, they were even ignorant of political realities.

Mamata lost her patience after being persistently denied a special package for Bengal. She directly charged the central government of discriminating against her state and being step-motherly towards it. She also sensed a conspiracy by the Congress High Command to break up the TMC by luring its MPs. The Congress was never sure of the reliability of the TMC's support and the year's political narrative was dominated by 'M' block of Mayawati and Mulayam propping up Manmohan with its biggest threats, Modi and Mamata, both suffering from the foot-in-mouth disease.

Mamata accused the Congress of using the CBI stick for political purposes. Political analysts felt that the CBI'S enquiry against K.D. Singh, the Trinamool Rajya Sabha MP, had triggered the outburst. The industrialist-turned-politician's name had featured earlier in the 2010 cash-for-vote controversy during the Jharkhand Rajya Sabha elections. He later on switched camps to join the Trinamool Congress and is a key TMC leader, tasked with the party's foray into states outside Bengal. Manmohan Singh believes in liberalization and Mamata is a shrill socialist. She called the UPA 'a rotten snail' and accused it of 'being comatose'.

'Mamata is not dependable. She is not trustworthy. This is the main issue,' said Shekel Ahmed, AICC general secretary and the man in charge of West Bengal, in an interview, weeks after the TMC pulled out of the UPA. Highly critical of the TMC, Shekel Ahmed said that while the Left look thirty-four years to lose popular support, the TMC was already losing the confidence of the people in merely a year and a half. 'Today, people are questioning their wisdom in bringing her to power. Echoing the line of his leader, Rahul Gandhi, Ahmed said there was no going back to the TMC; the Congress would fight elections on its own. People are disillusioned with both the TMC and the Left and this vacuum will only be filled by the Congress.' Ahmed smiled when asked if the Congress was breaking up the TMC. Given the Trinamool's own state of affairs, he said, there was no need to instigate a break up, it would implode naturally. If, for Mamata, the Congress was the bigger enemy Ahmed's comments also made it clear that for the Congress, Mamata was the bigger enemy than the Left.

However, newly appointed AICC General Secretary in charge of

West Bengal Dr C.P. Joshi, was soft on Mamata. He said, 'TMC has been our single largest coalition partner in the government, moreover, we have fought elections together for the Assembly in 2011.' He preferred to keep the door open for any future Congress—TMC relationship. The veteran Congress leader and AICC treasurer, Motilal Vora, was also very conciliatory. 'In politics, particularly between two parties, differences are inevitable but can be solved. In the interest of the country and democracy, Mamata will ultimately be on the side of the Congress', he was confident.

Mamata's other problem has been her clumsy handling of the media, making it difficult for her to improve her image. Instead of treating all sections of the media even handedly, including those critical of her, she set up her own media and tried to pit one section against the other. This has led to a polarization in the media with both sides losing credibility. The media supporting her tends to get isolated with other sections getting together and providing grist to the opposition mill.

So where does Mamata Banerjee stand today? Is the green beginning to fade, presaging the return of the red? It is too early to come to that conclusion. Mamata's own mistakes may have led to anger and disappointment but that does not mean that the people have forgotten the failures of the closing years of the Left Front rule. In fact, the TMC's narrow victory over the CPI(M) in the Howrah Lok Sabha by-election came as a warning to Mamata. It was the first election after the break-up of the Congress-TMC coalition. The TMC's Prasun Bandopadhyay, a popular footballer, polled 45 per cent of the votes, the CPI(M)'s Sudip Bhattacharya nearly caught up with 42 per cent and the Congress too polled over 10 per cent of the votes, making an anti-TMC total of over 50 per cent. Analysts say that though the TMC won the seat, it was not necessarily a victory. However, the CPI(M) claims that the rural voter was returning to the Left was premature. Thus, even if the green is showing clear signs of wear and tear and losing its sheen, the red is far from being emergent.

The chit fund scam that unfolded a few weeks before the Howrah election has had some impact on the rural vote. The state government desperately ignoring the state Election Commission's letters and its knee jerk reactions were seen as a ploy to delay the polls. Why would Mamata Banerjee be shy of holding rural polls with her rural support base more or less intact? The Saradha Group chit fund scam could have been a possible reason, with most of its ring leaders having direct and close TMC links. In rural areas, small savers had invested their life's earnings in these chit funds.

There were many more self-inflicted damages. The arbitrary arrest of a poor farmer, Shiladitya Chowdhury, who was promptly branded a 'Maoist' for interrupting Mamata's speech at Belpahari, in remote Jangalmahal, did not help her cause. The inability to deliver on the promise of 'poriborton' in villages, in terms of development and jobs, as well as the failure to get a settlement for the owners of Tata's Nano factory land has hurt sentiments. These may have been the TMC's pre-panchayat poll fears. In fact, asked about the chances of the TMC in panchayat elections, a veteran TMC member of Parliament said, '*pitiye jitbo*' (We will beat them up to win). Asked why the TMC needed to beat people up to win and whether their rural support base was dwindling, he arrogantly replied: '*Amra eto bochor onek maar kheyechi*' (We have been beaten up for so many years).

Mamata began her term with high expectations. Consider some laudatory comments by intellectuals and journalists: 'If there is one politician whose action matches her talk, it is Mamata Banerjee.' or 'Mamata is set to meet the aspirations of the people and bring about prosperity and developments that were denied so long.' (Jaideep Mazumdar); 'The change of guard has ignited fresh bout of optimism.' (Aparajita Gupta); 'It is time to leverage the state's inherent strengths and build brand West Bengal.' (Mousumi Ghosh, FICCI); 'She has achieved what she wanted to. She has to switch gears now.' (Prof. Prashant Mishra, IIM); 'Appropriate green energy projects can make us a world leader of solar energy environment of the whole world under the leadership of the new government.' (S.P. Gon Chaudhuri); 'With hopes of Bengal returning to its days of glory as a hub of educational excellence, the primary objective of Mamata's government is to free education institutions from the clutches of politics.' (Somdatta Basu). There were words of optimistic caution too: 'Bengal can bring back its days of glory provided there is governance, infrastructure, awareness and more.' (Dr Ajitava Roy Chaudhuri).

The land issue has always been and will be crucial in the days to come. It was the move to take over large areas of land in the rural areas for 'development' that led to the rural vote turning away from the Left Front and was a major factor in bringing Mamata and her TMC to power. By standing firm on her pledge not to allow forcible acquisition of land for industry, she has antagonized industry and a large section of the middle class. She has also antagonized a good section of the media, including the national media, as their market is the middle class. All indications, however, point to Mamata still retaining a major share of the rural vote and also the minority vote, considering that a very large section of the small and marginal farmers in West Bengal belong to the minority community.

The Saradha chit fund scam has undoubtedly dented her base somewhat but the peasantry will be suspicious of what the Left Front would do if it returns to power. Then again, Saradha grew from strength to strength during the Left rule. The question now is whether Mamata will stand firm despite the pressure from sections of the media and the middle and industrial classes or capitulate to them to win their goodwill. In the first case, she retains the rural vote but loses large sections of the urban vote. In the other the urban middle class may rally behind her but she stands a good chance of losing the rural vote. Can she strike a balance between the two positions and retain power? Only the future can tell.

With the Trinamool Congress government completing two years in power in the state, Finance Minister Amit Mitra released three booklets on the government's 'achievements in improving the economy of the state: the state achieved 7.6 per cent growth in GDP compared to the national average of 4.96 per cent during the financial year 2012-2013. Industry, the government claimed, grew at 6.24 per cent against the national average of 3.12 per cent. In agriculture, the state recorded 2.56 per cent against national growth rate of 1.79, while in service sector the state achieved 9.48 per cent against the national record of 6.59 per cent.

Reflecting on the challenges before her government, Mamata said: 'Two years are not a big time to evaluate a new government'. She pointed out that the revenue collection of Rs 32,000 crore for the fiscal 2012-13 was a record. In terms of expenditure incurred in the MGNREGA scheme, the state occupied the first position in the country. Her government 'had on its head the legacy of a long thirty-four year regime, a huge debt burden of more than Rs 200,000 crore and a completely crippled and demoralized government machinery,' she said. Of the revenue generated by the state, Rs 26,000 crore was being deducted by the centre 'directly from our accounts towards repayment of debts of the previous Left Front government. We could have ploughed back the entire money into development work,' she said.

The Chief Minister also claimed that her government was nearly successful in eliminating strikes and poor work culture in the east Indian state. 'We dedicate our achievements to Maa, Maati, and Manush of Bengal and once again resolve to do our best to make

Bengal the No. 1 state in the country.' Two years ago, she was seen walking her way to the state secretariat, Writers' Buildings, after taking the oath as the first woman Chief Minister of the state. Today, she is struggling to contain the grief of countless rural voters who have been betrayed by the Saradha chit fund scam. With the collapse of the Saradha chit fund, countless small investors who trusted the group believing it to have the state government's backing, are left in the lurch.

Two years is a good time to audit the delivery on promises by a government elected for a five-year term. In this case, one test is her success with delivering *poriborton* to the 1,57,41,720 voters who chose Mamata Banerjee as the new face of the state and rejected the thirty-four year CPI(M)-led Left Front regime. The promise of good governance and an end to 'autocracy and atrocities' was equally valid for the 1,03,26,180 voters who preferred the CPI(M) and its allies. The point is Mamata is being evaluated not just by her state but by the country and even leading world powers because she had democratically ousted a well-entrenched communist rule.

The point is that good governance need not necessarily be bad politics. Politics has acquired an unsavoury edge in West Bengal. Even listing perceptions of a cross section of people is likely to run into accusations of bias and attract such sobriquets as Maoist stooge. The student of the Presidency University, Tania Bharadwaj, Professor Ambikesh Mahapatra and the hapless farmer, Shiladitya Chowdhury, stand testimony to that. Yet the promise of *poriborton* demands that the astonishing claim at the end of the first year of Trinamool Congress rule that more than 90 per cent of the tasks listed by Mamata Banerjee for her term had been completed be put to test.

Good governance requires that the bureaucracy and the police function with perfect efficiency. The flagship promise of the Trinamool Congress presents a major delivery problem though. The land that was returned to the land losers of Singur through an ordinance followed by a legislation, a promise fulfilled as a tribute to the iconic struggle of the Ma, Mati, Manush banner, is still being held behind a brick wall. The court is yet to untangle the sloppy work by the government to restore the promised land to the land losers. Strictures passed by the Calcutta High Court on the quality of investigations into the killing of Kazi Nasiruddin in police custody and the transfer of the investigation to the Central Bureau of Investigation tell their own tale. Issues around efficiency, direction and oversight are obvious when different district courts take contrary positions on the conduct of police investigations into the biggest Ponzi scam, Saradha. That Mamata Banerjee has had to step in and sweep her possibly erring flock under her protective custody in the Saradha scam and other small and big trespasses implies that the problems of running a government and the party are beginning to overwhelm the party.

If governance was as picture perfect as promised, Mamata Banerjee would have no reason to describe various charges, from rape to assaults on journalists, as 'fabricated'. The observation by the West Bengal Governor M.K. Narayanan that a *'goonda raj'* had taken over in the immediate aftermath of the shooting and killing of a policeman during the election process at a local college is an indictment of the quality of governance. The fear that stalks women on the streets of Kolkata in particular and West Bengal in general, does not reflect a mere perception; it is based on data of reported crime. In governance and politics though, even perceptions matter and developments in the state require Mamata Banerjee to be on her guard, perpetually. She also needs to be able to deliver punches to her critics and the opposition with precision and power.

The snapping of ties with the Congress signalled the end of any scope and chance of industrial development of the state as Mamata Banerjee blaming her own industry ministry for the failure. The government's much delayed and half hearted announcements on industrial policy have evoked poor response from the business chambers. The new industry incentive scheme for large and medium scale industries has almost been ignored by the industrialists. The core committee set up for the purpose of regular dialogue with industrialists, earlier chaired by the industry minister is now being headed by Mamata Banerjee herself. There are no results to show for it though.

The tussle between the Tatas and the state government, after the Nano plant exit, caused biggest damage to the industrial image of the state. The upshot is that Mamata has not been able to fulfill her poll promise to farmers of Singur to return their land. There is more bad news on the industrial front. The exit of Haldia Bulk Terminal (HBT) a joint venture between ABG of Mumbai and LDA of France from the Calcutta Port Trust has proved to be a setback for the ailing port, according to its chairman, RPS Kahlon. There are reports of ESS Dec Aluminum, a major packaging unit owned by a Singapore based NRI, planning to quit the state too.

Relying more on the industry friendly image of the former FICCI Secretary-General, Amit Mitra, currently Finance Minister of West Bengal, Mamata Banerjee is making earnest efforts to invite investment from industrialists outside Bengal as well as international investors. Recently the pollution board cleared a coal-based methane project of Essar Oil, paving the way of additional investment of Rs 2,500 crore in the state. The Metro Corridor Extension Project held up for years is high on the Chief Minister's agenda. Quitting the railway portfolio at the centre has also hurt railway projects in the state. With a budget allocation of Rs 475 crore for four major projects by the former Congress's former Railway Minister, Pawan Bansal, against an allocation of Rs 10,000 crore by the earlier TMC minister holding the railway portfolio has endangered the future of these projects.

The state government is seeking to grant permission to the AMRI Hospital to re-open some departments. The government had ensured that almost all its directors were arrested and kept in jail after a devastating fire in December 2011, when ninety-one people choked to death. The Tata group's new chairman, Cyrus Mistry, is being duly and correctly cultivated. He recently, made the right 'never left Bengal, won't leave' comment even while remaining silent on Singur. Mamata, who never missed an opportunity to make sarcastic remark about 'Tata babu' is seeking to cozy up to the group through the urban development minister, Firhad Hakim, who says: 'We were never against Tata. The CPI(M) misguided him.'

The best analysis of West Bengal's failure to exploit its potential came from Ronen Sen, the former Indian Ambassador to the USA. He said, 'one of my regrets has been that over the decades I tried but I failed to get people to focus more on Bengal mainly due to lack of infrastructure, human potential, consistent land policy and presence of domestic players.' If you do not have domestic industry coming in here, you are not going to have foreign players coming in here".

Mamata's decision to politically rehabilitate her seven M.P.s—who found themselves out of work after the TMC's exit from the UPA—as advisors has spread only confusion at all levels of the government. One such advisor, attached to most important departments, said: 'As far as I know, I do not know.' Clearly, the team spirit is missing and governance has been the biggest casualty. Lack of co-operation from the state government is forcing the Kolkata-based National Green Tribunal to be shifted to Guwahati or Ranchi as per the directive of the Supreme Court. The state government's objection to the Supreme Court handing over the Saradha Case to the CBI is not improving its image. The continued confrontation with West Bengal Human Rights Commission over issues after issues has provoked the Commission to remark: 'the Honorable CM is a democratically elected popular leader. Even such a leader has to be abiding by Constitutional norms'.

The commission's Chairperson, Justice (Retd) Ashok Kumar Ganguly, expressed his displeasure over the Chief Minister branding farmer, Shiladitya Chowdhury, a Maoist, calling it a wild allegation. The panel asked the government to pay him compensation of Rs 2 lakh. Justice Ganguly in turn received a letter from government seeking clarification about his recent visit to Pakistan. The questions included, 'was permission taken', 'who funded', 'what was the purpose' and such others, in what is read as a desperate attempt to keep the retired Supreme Court Judge under leash.

Yes, as expected, the panchayat results have largely gone in favour of the TMC, re-confirming her continued hold over the rural voters. Mamata Banerjee is presently being expected to do better in the Lok Sabha polls, certainly adding to her tally of 19 MPs. The results of the next Lok Sabha elections may lead to re-alignment of political forces but that will only happen after the results are out, more based on arithmetic than issues and policies. Buoyed by her resounding victory in the Bengal Panchayat polls, when Mamata Banerjee recently launched the idea of a federal front on her Facebook page, it got immediate endorsement from Naveen Patnaik, Nitish Kumar, Akhilesh Yadav and Chandrababu Naidu. If the fifty-eight-year-old Chief Minister of West Bengal wins 30 Lok Sabha seats out of the 42—she won 19 in 2009—nothing can stop her from being the third largest party in 2014.

The closed door 'Bengal Beckons' industry meeting of 1 August

2013 in Mumbai, immediately after Mamata's victory in Panchayat Polls, was certainly more successful than similar interaction in New Delhi in December 2012 and from Bengal Leads in Haldia, West Bengal during early 2013.The perfect photo up of Mamata with a smiling Mukesh Ambani sitting beside her would go a long way in repairing the image of Brand Bengal, which took a beating after Tatas shifted the Nano out of Singur in 2008. Not only egged by successful Mumbai summit, Mamata was reportedly concerned about lack of industrial development in the state and was already planning to reshuffle her cabinet and also announce the West Bengal State Support for Industries Scheme 2013 with new incentives. She was only waiting for the Panchayat elections for announcing a pro-business industrial policy. However, it is not a coincidence that Mr Harsh Goenka, Chairman RPG Enterprises and one of the leading figures at Mumbai summit wrote an article entitled 'Zero Change from The Left' published in *The Times of India* only one day after the Mumbai summit echoing apprehensions in earlier paragraphs. The article read, 'After years once again, there was renewed hope—a hope of positive change—*poriborton.* What happened, unfortunately is far from encouraging. The sad truth is Bengal is back to square one with zero poriborton. Even though my Marwari mind shies away from investing in Bengal, my Bengali heart constantly seeks an opportunity to do so.' It is obvious Mamata will need much more than her personal charm to woo hard-nosed businessmen.

However, Mamata's handling of statehood agitation in Darjeeling shows that it is possible to deal with such stirs successfully without submitting to the politics of violence and blackmail. Her way of tackling the agitators stood in sharp contrast with the near total surrender of the previous Left Front Government. Even New Delhi may take a lesson or two from her.

The Bengal government has taken a significant step towards

restructuring the ailing transport sector by inviting bids for unutilized land at depots of transport corporation. This is the first time the Mamata Banerjee government is putting land on the block.

Intervening to end the deadlock affecting Damodar Valley Corporation's Thermal Power project in Purulia's Raghunathpur Industry Minister Partha Chatterjee said, 'At a time Chief Minister Mamata Banerjee is keen to attract investment to the State, there should not be disruptions.' Similarly the State government is pro-actively engaged in the sale of its stake in Haldia's Petrochemicals Ltd. to rescue its show-piece project from financial collapse.

In a changed tack Mamata has directed all departments to file status report on cabinet cleared projects since she came to power in May 2011. Tardy progress of the projects had irked Mamata and she commented 'criticizing the centre alone will not help.'

Governance requires cool and careful deliberation and certainly an absence of ad-hocism in decision-making and this vital lesson Banerjee has failed to imbibe in these two years. Hopefully, in the remaining three years, she will still change tacks for the better. Public memory is short and never mind the terrors of the left rule, continued failures on governance by the TMC will make it easier for the Left to make a triumphant return to the Writers' Building. This prospect West Bengal would certainly like to avoid but for that, Mamata Banerjee will need to bring about a real *poriborton.*

Acknowledgements

As with all such works, many discussions, readings, viewpoints and interpretations, etc. have had their part in the shaping of this book. However, as is often the case, space constraints prevent my personal written acknowledgement of every individual and inspirational source—and there have been many.

Having said that, I would particularly like to thank all those who agreed to speak to me both on and off the record; all of whom have not been individually identified.

I would also like to acknowledge the invaluable advice and encouragement of Aditi Roy Ghatak; Sankar Ray's support and Sneha Chatterjee's secretarial assistance. My thanks are also due to those who did not wish to be acknowledged.

I would also like to offer my heartfelt gratitude to Rupa Publications and its team, for their patience and help in bringing out this book.

www.ingramcontent.com/pod-product-compliance
Lightning Source LLC
LaVergne TN
LVHW091049080826
845145LV00002B/684